Dont bother me while Im calm

First published in Great Britain in 2002

10 9 8 7 6 5 4 3 2 1

Ebury Press
Random House, 20 Vauxhall Bridge Road, London SW1V 2SA

Random House Australia (Pty) Limited
20 Alfred Street, Milsons Point, Sydney, New South Wales 2061, Australia

Random House New Zealand Limited
18 Poland Road, Glenfield, Auckland 10, New Zealand

Random House (Pty) Limited
Endulini, 5A Jubilee Road, Parktown 2193, South Africa

The Random House Group Limited Reg. No. 954009

A CIP catalogue record for this book is available from the British Library

ISBN 0 091 88655 4

Photographs copyright © Geri Productions Limited; Dean Freeman; EMI
All photography by Dean Freeman, except pages 153-160 by Geri Halliwell and back
endpapers, row 4, images 2 and 3 by Andy Earle and Trudy Bellinger respectively

Art direction by Dean Freeman and Grace
Edited and designed by Grace

Printed and bound in Germany by Appl, Wemding

Papers used by Ebury Press are natural, recyclable products made from wood grown
in sustainable forests.

Geri Halliwell
Just for the Record
PHOTOGRAPHY BY DEAN FREEMAN

Spice Girls European tour 1998.

Round the world trip April 1999

hars my turn at?

let's talk about sex baby

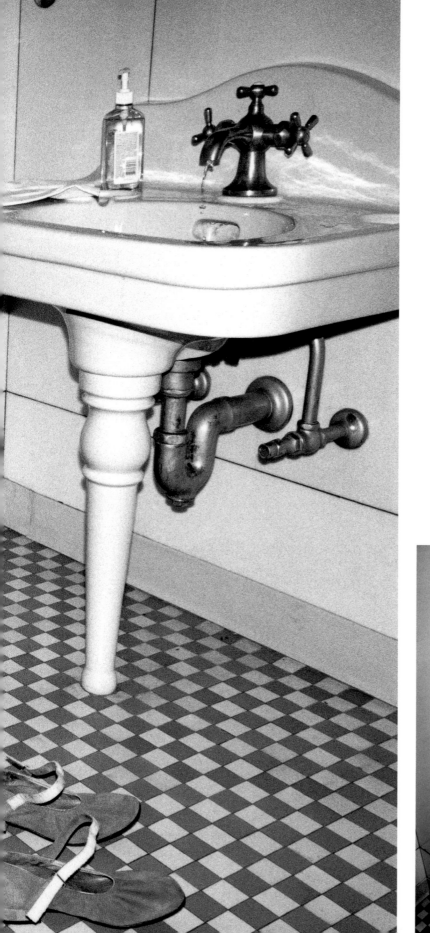

Prague 'look at me'
march 1999

something has to die in order to change.

me in my soap box as a UN
Goodwill Ambassador to the Philippines

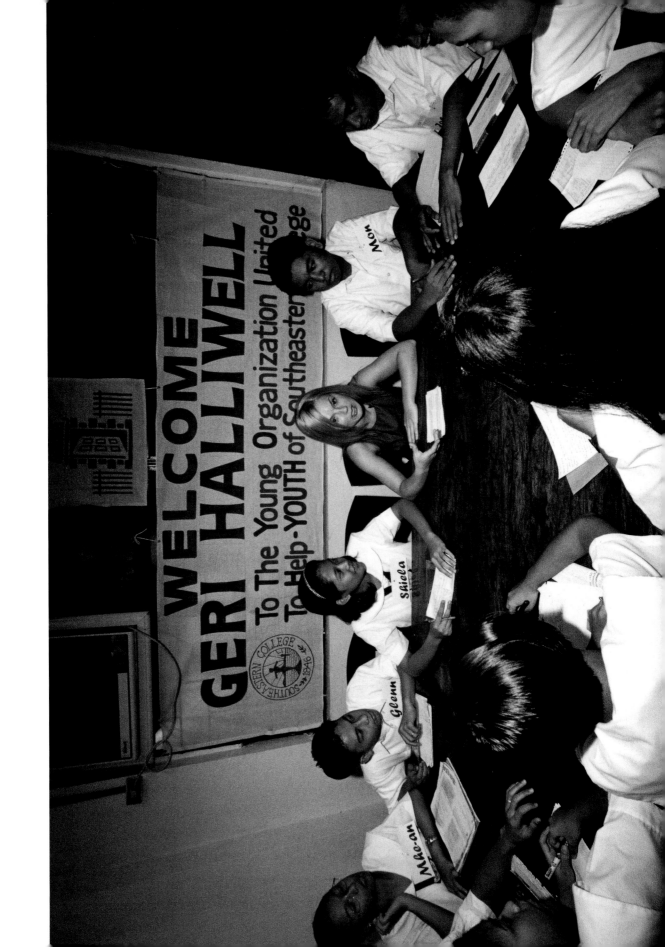

Chris Latino July 1999

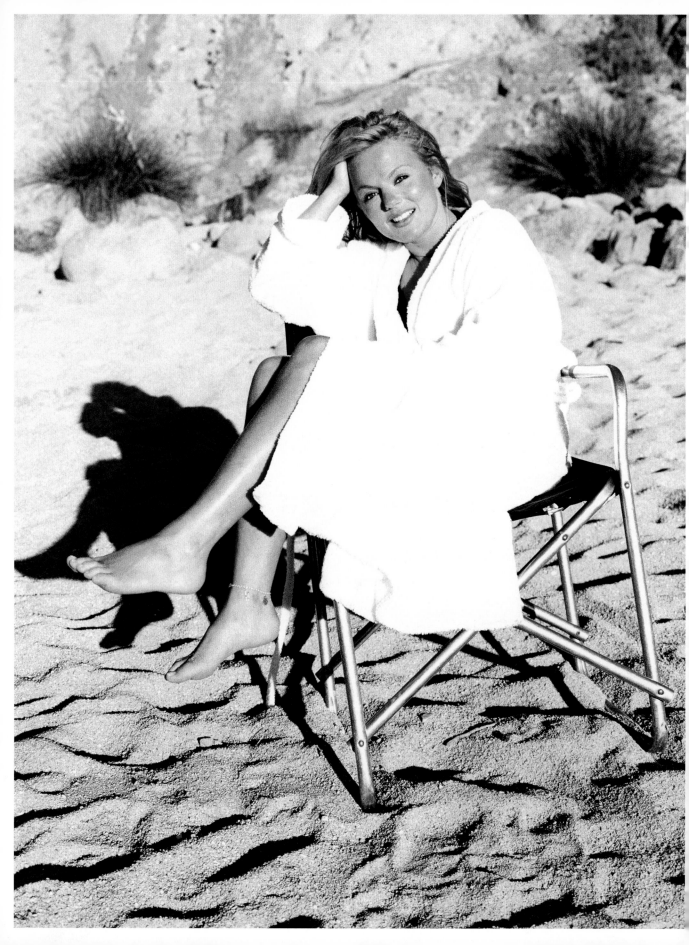

Ibiza Spain 2001

Don't call me stupid, stupid!

Miami - february 2001

Goodbye

Lying here in the warm sun it's easy to drift off. Staring up at a cloudless blue sky and surrounded by palm trees that shelter the sun-deck from prying eyes, I can imagine — just for a moment — that I'm on a secret fantasy desert island, miles from anywhere. Only the muffled noise of the traffic from Sunset Boulevard reminds me that I am here in my favourite hotel in Los Angeles, an oasis of calm in the heart of the city. I've been here before but this time it feels different. It's the perfect place to reflect on the journey that has brought me here and choose the path to follow next.

Ronnie has just brought me my lunch by the pool. When I moved into my villa — just set back from the main hotel in the manicured grounds — Ronnie came with the package. His job is to look after me and make me feel at home, so I suppose you could say he's done a pretty good job. He's very funny, *very* camp and loves to chat. Today's lunch is steamed fish, mustard mash and broccoli with some herbal tea to wash it down. Sometimes you just have to be grateful for the trappings of fame and, when it comes to Ronnie and a delicious meal by the pool, I can honestly say that I am.

I can't say that I came here intending to reflect on my life or even to stay very long. I was drawn to LA by other attractions. The first was the sunshine. I come alive in the springtime so, tired of waiting for the end of the English winter, I wanted to be somewhere warmer. I had professional reasons to be here too. I'd finished promoting my second album *Scream If You Wanna Go Faster* and I wanted to be where the action is. I had record producers to meet in LA and even some contacts to see in Hollywood.

When I got here I remembered that there was something else that attracted me to the city. Celebrities are ten a penny. Turn the corner and you bump into Christopher Walken making his way down the street with his shopping, go into a bar for a drink and there's Minnie Driver chatting to friends over lunch. Nobody points and nobody stares — in fact, in LA nobody *cares* and that's a relief. Last week, my sister Natalie came over to see me and we went to a theme park a few miles from town. We had a great time riding on the roller coaster and playing games on the stalls and we weren't disturbed by anyone. I can't see *that* happening at Alton Towers. I felt so happy. I felt free.

I got a call the other day from my manager, Andy. 'When are you coming back?' he asked. 'It's been a while now.'

'Oh,' I said. 'I'm not sure. I like it here. I think I want to stay a while longer.'

I could hear him sighing down the phone. 'OK,' he said, 'but Geri?'

'Yes, Andy?'

'Just make sure you don't get lost in La-La Land.'

I could see what he was worried about: here I was in Los Angeles miles from home and from the real world of Geri Halliwell — Pop Star. There's not much chance of stumbling across a copy of the *Sun* or the *Mirror* here or finding myself reading a magazine article with the headline IS GERI TOO SKINNY? I don't have to worry about walking down the street or going to the movies or popping to the shops. Here, I no longer have to deal with my fame. Maybe Andy was worried I was being swept up by the glitz and the glamour of the Hollywood social scene but that wasn't it at all. If I was getting lost it was in the opportunity to feel like a normal person again, to step back from the madness and reassess my life. Do I really want to work on that new record yet? Are movies the right way to go? I like it in La-La Land.

It's never as easy as that, though, is it? Something always comes along to bring you back down to earth and my something came along a little while ago as I was relaxing by the pool:

Monday 4th March 2002

Oh my God! was reading by the pool this morning, just relaxing when chris showed up and walked over to me. just came up for a friendly chat. first time I'd seen him in ages, over two years talk about blast from the past. Things move on and thats ok.

Everyone finds it embarrassing bumping into their ex but only the famous have the moment captured on film, sold to the press and discussed in the gossip columns. When Andy called to tell me that my meeting with Chris Evans and his new wife was all over the newspapers I was very shocked. Somehow somebody had managed to creep into the hotel and get the picture. It was terrible to realise that I wasn't even safe here but it also reminded me that in England it's like that every day of the week.

Chris hasn't been the only old friend to appear at my temporary home from home at the Sunset Marquis. Just last week I was walking upstairs to the villa when I bumped into another:

Friday 5th April 2002

Was on my way back from the pool bumped into Rob on the stairs. He's only staying in the villa directly below me! had a nice little chat both had such a busy few months it was great to see him out of the blue.

Apart from the unplanned meetings, I've spent most of the time here on my own, like some old movie star in self-imposed exile. So it was great having Natalie over last week. We had a fantastic time shopping and taking day trips out of town and I even took her to the *Vanity Fair* party after the Oscars. It was so much fun because everyone was there and she loved seeing people like Oprah Winfrey and Tom Hanks. Now, though, even she's starting to wonder when I'm coming home.

'You can't live in a hotel for ever,' she said as we sat in a café after an exhausting shopping session.

'I know,' I replied. 'That's why I was wondering if you fancied coming and having a look for an apartment with me.'

And that's what we did. It didn't take long to find a perfect little place in a secluded spot a few minutes down the road. It looks like my days lying by the pool and drinking Ronnie's herbal tea are over, but it feels exciting to be moving somewhere a little more permanent. My life is at a crossroads in every way — career, home, family, fame — and this city 5,000 miles from home seems the best place to work out which way to turn next.

First of all, though, I have to understand how I got this far.

·

For me, the Spice Girls were more than *just* a pop band. In many ways they were my family, my personal support system.

Six months before I joined the group my father had died, suddenly, of a heart attack at the age of 72. Dad had always encouraged me to follow my dreams and was my greatest fan. His death left me feeling robbed, hurt and angry. I spent the months after his death in a daze. I sank into a depression so deep I wasn't sure I'd survive it.

The group offered me hope in this darkness: the hard work, the grand plans and the fun we had together allowed me to lock my problems away for a while. We became a family as much as a band. We even spent our early days living together. We were five girls in a three-bedroom house in Maidenhead queuing outside the bathroom for hours in the morning, sharing clothes and make-up tips and, most of all, working hard to make our dreams come true. Every day the five of us would pile into my little Fiat Uno and go to the rehearsal studio to work on our singing and our dance routines. We really were five wannabes and our success was built on a foundation of love and support. That closeness filled the empty space I had felt inside since my dad's death.

I could understand why the world was so confused about my decision to leave because I wasn't too clear about it myself. There were good reasons why it happened when it did but, even though they were important, the more I think about it now, the more I realise they only tell part of the story.

The girls and I always knew that a band like the Spice Girls would one day outstay its welcome on the bedroom walls of Britain's teenagers. A group like ours needed to know the right time to call it quits and, in the early days, we talked about giving it our best shot for two years then getting out before we were past our sell-by date. At the time, two years seemed a long way off in the future and when we thought about the band's shelf life we never imagined what a phenomenon we would turn out to be.

By November 1997, the two-year mark didn't seem so far away anymore and it began playing on my mind. At the same time the Spice Girls' insane schedule had taken its toll on me and my eating disorders had returned. My response was typical: I thought I could fix my internal problems by changing something external, which was why I thought we should part company with our manager Simon Fuller. Looking back Simon was a wonderful manager and I wouldn't be where I am today without him but, at the time, I believed that we needed a change. For a while it felt great that the girls and I were in control again. It was just like the old days in my Fiat Uno: five girls taking on the world. The downside was that, without Simon, taking on the world was a tiring business. It was ironic that we had sacked him because of our heavy workload but now we were working twice as hard to prove we didn't need his help.

I'd been thinking for some time that the Spice Girls should go out with a bang rather than a fizzle. One wet night in Frankfurt in early March 1998, on the tour coach on the way to yet another hotel, I blurted out that I wanted our Wembley show in September to be our last — a grand finale in front of our home fans.

I wanted to box it up in a nice neat package. The girl band thing conquered. Mission accomplished.

Their silent response told me the girls had other ideas. I suppose I hoped the others would agree with me but they made it very clear that my departure would not be the end of the Spice Girls. They wanted to carry on. It was their group as much as mine and it was only fair that the majority should have their way. I could understand how they felt too. When something was working so well, why would you want it to end?

So why did I want the best thing that had ever happened to me to end? When the girls said they would carry on without me, I still knew I wanted to get off the roller coaster at the end of the tour. I hoped that the other girls would understand that this was the right decision for me and that things could return to something like normal until then. In the end, it didn't work out like that. Maybe the others felt as if I was abandoning them and they drew closer together. It was natural, really. We were preparing for different futures. I just hoped I could hang on for another six months, fulfil my obligations and say goodbye to the fans in my own way. That was all very well in theory but then something happened that, at the time, seemed to bring things to a head.

When I was eighteen, I was getting dressed in my little flat above a shop in Watford one morning when I noticed a small, hard lump in my right breast. I wasn't too concerned at first but I went to see my doctor, expecting to be told it was nothing to worry about. Instead, I was admitted to Watford General Hospital for an operation. They wanted to remove the growth and run tests to check if it was cancerous. I never really thought about breast cancer or the risk of losing a breast. When you're that young you think you are invincible and I suppose I just assumed everything would be OK. I couldn't really grasp the significance of what was happening to me at the time, but when the results came back negative a few days later, the sense of relief was enormous.

In May 1998, I learnt that the press were planning to run with the story of my teenage operation. I knew the story would come out one way or the other so I decided it would be better to take things in hand and speak to the press myself. That way the whole thing might be dealt with more sensitively and I would have the chance to make some serious points about the issue. I had just read the heartbreaking story of the journalist Ruth Picardie, a mother of two who died of breast cancer at the age of 32. Her book had moved me deeply and made me realise how lucky I had been. I saw it as a chance to give a wake-up call to other young women.

Although some might think it was just a slogan or a gimmick, I had always been serious about 'Girl Power' and felt that the Spice Girls were on a mission to save girls and lift their self-esteem. When I started focusing on breast cancer awareness I saw how all these things were connected, and when I was invited onto *News at Ten* to discuss my experiences I was delighted to agree. This could save lives, after all.

Unfortunately, the girls made it clear that they would rather I waited until after I left in September before giving the interview. I worked myself up into a state about it. At that moment, the band seemed less important to me than saving the lives of young women by raising breast cancer awareness. I was faced with a choice — stay until September and turn down the interview or leave the band now.

I remember saying to myself that this was not just about money or staying in nice hotels or being a celebrity, it was also about making a difference. The answer was obvious — it was time for me to go. That night at home in the little farm cottage in Hertfordshire where I was living I wrote in my diary: 'I have loved and lost. I give up. My heart is breaking.' There was to be no American leg of the tour for me, no farewell at Wembley and no more Ginger Spice.

At the time, and for a long while afterwards, it seemed to be as simple as that — the breast cancer interview had forced my hand and I had no choice but to leave. As time went on, though, I came to realise that while that issue *was* important, it was only one part of the picture.

Deep down in my heart of hearts I know that the disagreement about the interview was a life raft I used to get out of the group. In a way I was looking for a reason and that was the one that came to hand. I found it easier to talk about other issues and to focus on other things rather than face up to myself and how I was feeling. I'd always found it really difficult to say, 'You're hurting me', but if I ever saw someone or something else suffering, something external, I'd find it much easier to stand up for them than myself.

The situation I was in was more a relationship breakdown than an argument of principle over one particular issue. In the end I think the actual situation itself was irrelevant. Recently a friend was telling me about an argument she had with her husband about one of them putting glasses in the dishwasher. They were absolutely flipping out about it and obviously it had got absolutely nothing to do with why they were annoyed with each other. It was the same with the girls and me. Of course they cared about the issue too. How they felt about breast cancer or how I felt about breast cancer had absolutely jack shit to do with my departure. It was the glass in the dishwasher, that's all, and it could have been something else entirely.

I am grateful for the time I have had sitting in the California sunshine trying to come to terms with the choices I have made in my life. Leaving the Spice Girls has always been one of the most difficult for me to understand. I suppose, for a long time, I didn't really want to address it at all.

I have always based my actions on instinct. It's quite a childish approach, you might think, but if I feel I need to do something I just do it without thinking the reasons through.

The thinking comes later.

One thing that *was* clear at the time I decided to leave was that inside Ginger Spice, underneath the make-up, the big hair, the giant platforms and the headline-grabbing dresses, there was a real girl and she was being suffocated.

The Ginger character was my own invention, of course, and did represent a side of me which, for a while, was a lot of fun. Although I was in my early twenties when I joined the group I was always a late developer — I didn't have my first period until I was seventeen and my boobs seemed to appear overnight at the same age — so I went through a late puberty during my years with the Spice Girls. Some people go through a punky phase — I went through Ginger and, for a while, I liked it. It was like putting on a uniform. You don't have to think, you don't have to deal with being a human being, and that was perfect for a vulnerable young woman who didn't want to feel anything.

I was going through so many changes that it was natural that a different person would come out of the Spice Girls to the girl who went in. By the time my four years was up, I was completely different.

Ginger had served her purpose and deadened my pain for a while but now I was over her. In the end, I was just putting on a uniform I had outgrown six months or a year before I finally decided to take it off.

'Musical differences' is the classic reason given when a band splits up and they did play their part for me too. I have always loved pop music and, while I can appreciate other styles like rock or dance or r'n'b, in my heart I have always been a pop music girl. Right at the beginning of the Spice Girls, the boss of the record company, Ashley Newton, had tried to turn us into an r'n'b group. He sent 'Wannabe' over to America to be remixed by some hot r'n'b producers. He brought us jungle versions and hip-hop mixes and I hated them all. Although Mel B was a big fan of r'n'b, she agreed with me that these versions just didn't work so we exercised our Spice veto! The single was released in its original, poptastic form and went to Number One.

But it became obvious to me that the others would want to move in that direction in the future and I knew I didn't want to go there with them. I've always been very pop-orientated; I like melodies more than grooves and for me that's the difference. Pop is about songs and r'n' b is about tracks. The simple truth is that I didn't share their vision. The others felt that they could take the group somewhere else but I couldn't see it and sometimes you have to step aside and let people be who they want to be. It made sense to me to let them go and let them grow in the r'n'b direction they loved. And, as it turns out, that was exactly what they did.

The only person I know who really understands how I felt at the time I left the Spice Girls is staying in the villa below me here in my LA hideaway at the Sunset Marquis. Robbie Williams knows how relationships work inside a successful band and how it feels to leave one behind because he experienced it when he left Take That. Being in the Spice Girls was like being in a marriage. The relationship between the five girls in the group was as close and intense as a love affair, with all the highs and lows that go with that. But a marriage only has to accommodate two people and we had to find a way to keep all five of us happy.

We were five young girls full of hormones, under extreme amounts of pressure and with different kinds of egos and personalities. It was inevitable that we were not going to get on all the time. At the start of a relationship you fall in love and think the other person is the bee's knees. You think they are going to save you from your wretched self and that you will live happily ever after.

I remember those days with the girls with love and affection. Mel C and I shared a childlike fascination for pop music and the dream of making it. Emma was the little sister I never had and I idolised her for it. Victoria and I had an equal and quite grown-up relationship. We understood each other and I thought she was a very smart cookie and very funny.

Mel B and I were real buddies, always getting into trouble together. When the two of us were in our heyday, people would be horrified and delighted at the same time by our behaviour. We were like two Tasmanian devils bursting into the room, climbing on the table and dominating everything and everyone. It was very, very contagious and very strong.

The closeness of the relationships in the band was the foundation of our success but by the end we had started to squabble. Things were far from perfect and I have to take responsibility for my part in that.

A lot of successful people have very similar CVs — maybe a dead parent, a broken home, poverty, a sense of physical inadequacy. And these are all things that make you want to get out there and prove yourself. My childhood wasn't exactly the Waltons but whose is? While I was in primary school, my parents' marriage ended in divorce. With my father dying 6 months before I joined the group I had so much drive, energy and passion for the Spice Girls because I felt as if I had it all to prove.

From day one I had always put all my energies into the band. I was full of creative ideas and I refused to accept defeat, play by the rules or take second best. I was persistent to the point of annoyance! If someone told me something couldn't be done it would be like a red rag to a bull. I'd see it as a challenge.

I think that many of us like to have partnerships with people who we can control. It is very hard to find a balanced relationship whether personal, business or creative. Some people like to be passive but some of us want to be the dominators. No prizes for guessing who wanted to be the dominators in the Spice Girls! Mel B and I very quickly assumed the leadership roles soon after we got together.

For the most part, these aspects of my personality were a definite bonus for the group but at the same time my dominant role actually reflected my weakness rather than my strength. I felt so out of control inside that I tried to take control of anything external, whether it was my weight, other people or situations we found ourselves in as a group.

Looking back, I sometimes overstepped the boundaries.

As the band's success grew things started to change and the leadership role I had played didn't seem so necessary anymore. The Spice Girls had become a machine and we weren't driving it, it was driving us. The machine was bigger than the five of us and didn't need any emotional attachment or soul to run any more. The wheels were turning and I wasn't controlling the momentum. Without that control, I wasn't sure why I was needed. I began to feel so useless that I would desperately try to regain the power I had had — even if that meant sabotaging things.

When I think about it now, I can see that this was going on as far back as the time we parted company with Simon Fuller. I absolutely adored Simon and he was crucial to our success but there was a tension in our relationship. A big factor in Simon's departure was me sticking my fingers up at him because I saw him as a father figure. There was a problem with the heavy schedule he had put the group on, but it was also about me playing the defiant, silly little teenager who wanted to be free and do it her way.

I tried to be the strong one in the Spice Girls even though, inside, I was just as scared as everyone else that things would go wrong and I'd fall flat on my face. At home when I was a young child and Mum and Dad were splitting up, I'd always played the role of mediator, Little Miss Fix-It trying to hold things together. I knew how to manipulate and calculate to get my needs met, and I learnt to read people very well. There's still a side of me that wants to reassure everyone that everything's OK, a side of me that won't let me admit my true feelings.

My family life taught me that reconciliation wasn't possible in life, only confrontation. I didn't know how personal or working relationships could survive when people disagreed or argued because my role models hadn't taught me how. I didn't want confrontation but it seemed inevitable if there was any sort of problem because I had no idea how to discuss things constructively.

I had good reasons to leave the group, but I was ill-equipped emotionally to work through the problems with the others and explain how I felt or find a compromise or solution. Things weren't right and my instinct had been to make a move — any move. Rather than sit down and talk about things I had cried and bawled like a baby and thrown my toys out of the pram. Sometimes the only way to feel in control is to take action, whether that is spoiling a relationship or finishing a relationship. It's not about the quality of that relationship or whether it needs to end or not, it's about regaining control. And that is exactly what I had done.

So the reasons for my departure were a mixture of all these things. Part of it was about my belief that the group should go out on top, part of it my feelings about Ginger and the musical differences that were emerging in the group, but the split was also about relationships and my sometimes destructive attempts to keep control at any price.

My departure from the Spice Girls was sudden and the timing was far from ideal. The girls had to finish the last of their European concerts before starting their first American tour. The newspapers were full of speculation about the financial implications for all of us if the tour collapsed. I knew otherwise, though, because I knew how well the girls would respond to the added pressure my absence would create. They could make it without me.

Even though the timing was far from perfect, the fact remains that I had reached a point where I could not have continued.

I did a runner.

Some people run off before they get married. Call me a commitment-phobe, the sort of person who has a fear of intimacy when the going gets tough, but that was where I was at that time. There is never really a right time to make a break and leave, whatever the situation. I can rationalise and reason but the fact is I did a runner. And I'm not proud of it.

I could beat myself up for the rest of my life about my departure from the group but as I sit here in LA, mulling it all over, I have tried hard to take a more balanced view. We were all responsible for the state of our relationships inside the group and my motivation for walking out was not purely selfish. I had felt that leaving was the decent thing and that it would have been disloyal to stay on for the wrong reasons. I could have stayed and gone for the easy ride, turned up and put a mask on. I could have pretended everything was fine but would that be honest to the twelve-year-old girl who bought our records or tickets to our shows? Our fans really did believe in us and we owed them honesty at the very least.

As much as my ego found it hard to accept, I knew it would be great for the girls to carry on as a four-piece. At the same time, being in a band is like being in a nest — eventually you want room to open your wings and see if you can fly on your own. Deep down, I had always wanted to go solo, but it took courage to admit it and even more to give it a try. When I left, everyone told me I was mad to walk away. These days they congratulate me and tell me how smart I was to get out.

Inside my heart, though, I'm not proud of leaving when I did. I'm not proud about that at all.

.

The separation between us was pretty much total. They had the tour to get on with and I needed to have a cut-off period. I had such strong, different relationships with all four that I felt I had to make sure I got the clean break I needed. It's like when you finish with a boyfriend, you're never going to get a new one unless you put the old one down. I had to make room in my life and it was painful to both parties but it had to be done. I needed to face my demons on my own and they needed to work out how to be a four. How could they do that if I kept on popping my head up and saying 'Hi guys, I'm still around'?

Just like any relationship it wasn't just the breaking up that was hard to do — the aftermath was pretty painful too. It felt as if a part of me had been removed, like I'd had an arm or a leg chopped off, because the group and the girls were such an important part of my life. Something magical had ended and I felt a tremendous sense of loss. I knew that I had made it happen and had wanted it to end but that didn't stop me missing the girls. They had been my family for four years.

In late September, the Spice Girls performed the final date of their world tour at Wembley Stadium. It was a beautiful warm autumn evening and I went for a walk outside in the fields behind the cottage where I was staying just as the sun was setting. I couldn't help imagining the scene at the stadium where the fans would be gathering, some of them believing the rumours that I would come on as a special guest for one last hurrah. It would have been wonderful if it had been true but this was no time for comebacks. I would have loved the chance to say goodbye to the fans who had given me so much, but it was not to be. It was a difficult night.

A few days afterwards, I went to stay at George Michael's house in the South of France near St Tropez. George and his partner Kenny Goss were friends and offered me their support as soon as I left the group. Their home was always open when I needed some comfort and company. I could kick off my shoes and try and relax, away from the glare of the cameras.

During my stay at George and Kenny's I heard that Victoria and David were staying at Elton John's house near Nice. I decided to give Victoria a call. It was the first time we had talked since my departure but I was so pleased to speak to her and let her know I was nearby. After chatting for a while, we ended up deciding to meet for dinner that night, so she and David called over to the house and we all went out to have a meal at a local restaurant.

I have no idea how they knew but by the time George, Kenny and I arrived at the restaurant, there were already paparazzi waiting. They must have thought Christmas had come early because it was quite a line-up — a Spice Girl, an ex-Spice Girl, a pop megastar and his boyfriend and a superstar footballer. Word spread fast and pretty soon the place was surrounded. It was a nightmare. But it was lovely to see Victoria and David again and, once we were inside, we had a really enjoyable and mellow evening and caught up on the four months since I had left. At the end of the night we couldn't get out of the door for flashing cameras and that part of it was horrendous. In retrospect, I wish we had stayed at home that night but I was very happy that we'd met up and had a chance to talk. I have real affection for Victoria and David.

In the next few months I had what I call my 'Spice Girl Moments'— times when I was reminded of what we shared together or when I realised that it was really over. One day, a few months after I left the group, I was working with the stylist Kenny Ho — who I had known since my days with the girls and who was still working for them — when I noticed a beautiful golden shoe in Kenny's bag.

'Oh, they're nice shoes, Kenny,' I said eagerly. 'Are they for me?'

Kenny looked a bit hesitant before telling me: 'Sorry, Geri. Those are actually for Victoria's dummy at Madame Tussauds. I'm going there later so they can fit them.'

I think Kenny knew it would hurt my feelings and didn't really want to tell me but it seemed to bring it home: I wasn't in the Spice Girls any more. I remember feeling really left out. It took that beautiful golden shoe for me to realise it was really over.

It was very strange seeing the group performing without me. It was like seeing your ex-husband with another woman — you don't want to be with him any more but you'd like to think he still loves you. Part of me, the ego part, wanted confirmation that I was needed in the band. The bigger and better part of me wanted them to do well. After all, I'd helped create the Spice Girls and even I liked to think they would go from strength to strength.

I will always love the girls and I am so grateful for what they and the fans gave to me. We were together for four years but we crammed twenty years of experience into that time. I dream about the two Melanies, Emma and Victoria all the time and there's not a day goes by when they aren't in my mind.

At the end of that year, six months or so after I left, the girls were back at the top of the Christmas charts with 'Goodbye'. It seemed like business as usual. The song seemed to be on the radio all the time. I'd hear it when I was driving in my car, at home in my kitchen or working out at the gym and every time I did it would make me cry because I would feel so nostalgic and sad. It felt as if they were singing it to me. Nobody likes goodbyes but there it was — a goodbye song — and what else was there really left to say?

It was hard to remember how life had been before I walked into that first audition and began this extraordinary journey but now the most important, successful and rewarding period of my life had ended. I knew I had to move on but I felt lost. For four years I had been consumed by the Spice Girls but now the other four were distant voices singing to me from the radio and visible only on the TV screen. I hadn't only lost my best friends and my career, I had also lost myself.

Without Ginger to hide behind, I wasn't really sure who Geri was any more.

Knock Down Ginger

It was too late to back out now. I was in the green room, where they put the guests while they are waiting to go into the studio, at the BBC's *Parkinson* show, going crazy with nerves and worry. I was about to undergo my first big public interview since leaving the Spice Girls. I suppose you could say I'm drawn to danger or that I get off on fear because this was hardly a gentle comeback. There I was waiting to appear on TV's biggest chat show in front of an audience of millions! Bang! Welcome back, Geri! This was not a nice and gentle *Smash Hits* interview or an easy ride on a daytime TV sofa. This was hardcore. What the hell was I doing?

I sat there, fidgeting, terrified, waiting to go on. I was dreading the interview because I was so worried that Parky would give me a grilling about the reasons why I had left the band. It was January 1999, eight months after my departure, but I still felt very raw and very nervy. I knew he had a job to do and any interviewer worth their pay cheque would ask the question everyone wanted to know the answer to: 'So, Geri, why did you really leave the Spice Girls?' And Parky was the best in the business.

I had had a chance to sit down and chat about the interview with him earlier in the day and explained how vulnerable I felt. I hoped that we had found a balance between him doing his job and getting what he needed and me feeling comfortable. In the end, we agreed that we would touch on the subject but that he would respect my boundaries and not go too far. We said he could touch on my departure but he promised to be a gentleman and use his instinct. I was reassured but knew that once I was sitting in that chair there would be no escape. Anything could happen.

That night I decided to wear my black polo neck and my black skirt. Black is understated but it says everything. I wear black when I'm feeling non-committal and undecided and when I don't want the world to look at me because I'm feeling fat. My family had come along to the show and I was in my dressing room when they arrived. They knew I was nervous and wanted to offer me some support and I remember my mum and my brother Max poking their heads round the door saying, 'You alright?' The trouble was that they were even more nervous than I was and they ended up making me feel more anxious!

The other guests that night were Dawn French and Carol Vorderman. Dawn's a really good friend, so it was a relief that she was on the show, although I didn't know Carol. I was the last one on and as I waited I watched the show coming through on the TV monitor. Hearing Parky in action was making me even more nervous but his interview with Dawn was fine and I started to feel a bit better. That was before his interview with Carol began.

There had been reports in the paper about Carol's relationship with her father and Parky asked her about it.

'Do you see your father any more?' he asked.

Carol didn't look too pleased with the question.

'Well, I don't really want to talk about it,' she answered.

I thought Parky would leave it at that but, being the interviewer he is, he didn't. Instead, he came back with the same question or a new version of the same question three times. There I was in the green room, which felt like my holding-pen, getting a taste of the treatment I could expect in a few minutes, time and I started freaking out. Carol was looking pretty uncomfortable but I was going into a complete panic — Oh my God, it's my turn next! What's he going to do to me?

My appearance on *Parkinson* was a turning point for me. The eight months between my departure from the Spice Girls and my first real step back into the limelight had been frightening but exhilarating. When I left the group, part of my leaving agreement was not to talk to the press for the first few months. As well as giving the girls breathing space to be a foursome, which I felt was really important, it gave me time to just reflect and keep my mouth shut about the reasons for my departure and protected me from saying something I might later regret.

When I had first left the group I had been offered half a million pounds to sell the story to *Hello!* magazine but I was obliged to turn them down. I didn't speak to journalists for months after I left. I think it was really important that I didn't talk. You need distance and a bit of a cooling-off period. I wanted to tell my story in my own time and wait until I was ready, and that meant writing it myself.

In retrospect, taking on a project as time-consuming and emotionally draining as a book (*If Only*, as it came to be called) was not the most sensible thing to do at that point in my life. I was feeling really lethargic and tired every day. The last four years — in the eye of the Spice Girls storm — had caught up with me. I was absolutely exhausted. I was also feeling more than a little lost.

It was all very well deciding that I wasn't Ginger any more, but who was I? I had taken the Ginger Spice uniform off but I didn't really know what I was going to find underneath. I was so used to being two-dimensional with a switched-on smile and a cheery 'Hi!' that I didn't know how to just be me. I had to build myself back up layer by layer. The Ginger years had been times of tremendous internal change for me and I was coming out of my delayed adolescence and losing my teenage bravado. When you are a teenager, you think you know it all and then, when you realise you don't, you are in trouble. Now, without Ginger to hide behind, my confidence would have to come from somewhere else.

I also had to find a new external identity because after all my years in uniform I wasn't actually sure what I wanted to look like! Wearing a lot of black was my way of avoiding the decision. I didn't want to be the homely girl and I didn't want to be ladylike. I didn't want to be anything.

At the same time I was undergoing one of the most extraordinary and significant experiences of my life, allowing filmmaker Molly Dineen to come into my world to make a documentary about Geri's life after Ginger.

Molly Dineen had a reputation as one of the most inventive and hard-hitting documentary makers around. She had a real gift for getting under the skin of her subjects whether they happened to be the British army, Tony Blair or the bosses, zookeepers and animals at London Zoo. At one stage, there had been a real chance that the next pillar of British society to get the Dineen treatment would be its biggest pop band — the Spice Girls.

During the early days of the Spice Girls' world tour, our manager Nancy had suggested that it would be a good idea to meet Molly to talk about a behind-the-scenes documentary she'd like to make with us. So she came along to meet us in the dressing room one evening and we got talking and immediately hit it off. I thought she was fascinating.

It was obvious from chatting with her that the kind of documentary Molly wanted to make would be raw and real. That wasn't going to happen with the Spice Girls! We were at the height of being five cartoon characters and it made no sense to blow the mystique or glamour of the group for the eight-year-olds who idolised us. We were like superheroes to those fans and it was very easy to keep it that way. Why spoil it for them? And why spoil it for us, for that matter?

The last thing we wanted to think about at the time was a documentary. We were so busy and all we could really think about was going on stage or getting to the next venue. So we couldn't be bothered with it. In fact, we didn't even discuss it properly. The time just wasn't right.

In the summer of 1998, shortly after I left the group, I was staying at George and Kenny's Los Angeles home when I got talking with a stylist friend of George's called Kim Bowen. Kim had worked with the Spice Girls on the 'Say You'll Be There' video and it turned out that Molly was her best friend. It seemed to be a very weird coincidence and it planted the idea in my mind of getting in touch with her again, so I gave her a call.

I had already started things off by recording a video diary on a camcorder but I loved the idea of Molly taking the project over. We decided that she would follow me for the next three months of my life — the first outside the Spice Girls — in private and public for every waking moment.

Part of the appeal of the documentary was that it gave me something to occupy my time. Leaving the Spice Girls was very hard to adjust to. I was freaking out because I had no purpose any more, having basically made myself redundant. I was wondering what the hell I was going to do with my life and whether I was going to be unemployed for ever.

When I was in the Spice Girls I was used to being on camera the whole time and obviously I hadn't got over that yet! I suppose there was some narcissism going on but I was also looking to understand myself and what had happened to me.

Perhaps self-indulgently, I also thought that viewers would be fascinated! Wouldn't they want to know what happens to a girl who had been through the sort of change that I had and how she would cope with her new life? I had been in this cocoon for four years but to me it felt like ten because it was so intense. I had been living and breathing the Spice Girls every day. Everything was done for me and all my needs were catered for. Then suddenly everything stopped. Imagine if you were living in a bustling, busy city street and being removed and plonked into the middle of the jungle. This could obviously be good material for a compelling piece of film. Having said that, I hadn't really thought through just how compelling it was likely to become.

With the Spice Girls, when I was on camera, I was keeping up an image of happy Geri no matter how I was really feeling. Even though camera crews were always there, they never made demands on me beyond a smile and a joke and, when I was having a private moment, they would leave me alone. It wasn't like that with Molly Dineen.

Molly was not a woman who was going to stand for me being switched 'on' for the camera in any shape or form. It's not like networking a room at a party, which you can do for an hour but you can leave and sit down and talk with your real mates. You can't keep all that shallow smiley-smiley behaviour up for months on end. I couldn't even sustain it for a week. Within a few days she broke me and all of a sudden I realised I'd woken up to my biggest nightmare. I felt like this stupid specimen that was being examined and prodded like one of the animals she'd filmed in London Zoo. In the end I said to her, 'Molly, I am not an elephant!' and I remember thinking: What have you got yourself into here, Geri? You can't do this. I really felt like I'd completely stitched myself up.

Part of me went into a panic and wanted to pull the plug on the whole thing there and then but I had committed to the project and to Molly so how could I, no matter how worried I was? And how would that look to people? At the same time, I was lonely, desperately lonely. I had been out of touch with my mates from Watford who all had their own lives to worry about. I had also lost four of my best friends and at the same time, tax reasons meant I could only go home for a limited amount of time. So, sad as it sounds, I really didn't have a lot else going on. Molly was great company and I just thought I'd hang out with her.

There is a very funny scene in the final documentary where Molly and I are on the Eurostar and she is filming me as I speak to my lawyer in the UK. He was understandably worried about the implications of the project so I reassured him by saying that I had 'complete control, and if there's anything bad in it we'll edit it out'. Molly told me there and then that she wouldn't be wasting her time if that was the arrangement and I realised she was right.

In the end we made a deal — I handed over 50 percent of control to her but retained the other half myself. This was a huge step for me because with the Spice Girls we had 99 percent control of imagery and everything that went out with our names or faces on it. In practice, though, I realised that if you're going to let an artist express themselves you cannot even sensor them that much. So I took a huge risk and let Molly do her thing. I decided that if it wasn't going to be just a Geri Halliwell commercial I had to let it go and allow Molly to do her work. So long as it didn't destroy my career, then that was OK! The problem was that I couldn't have picked a worse time to submit myself to Molly's all-seeing eye.

OK, so Molly captured some wonderful times like when I sold off my collection of Ginger Spice outfits at Sotheby's, and when I sang 'Happy Birthday' to Prince Charles on his 50th birthday at the Lyceum Theatre.

She was also there to record me jumping up and down on the hotel bed singing 'New York, New York' on the night before my debut at a press conference as UN ambassador. Looking back on that first UN press ordeal with all these serious people with their difficult questions makes me feel proud. I'm just a girl from Watford. I wouldn't say I'm highly intelligent, I haven't got degrees and honours, but I'm not stupid and I have a hungry mind and I do care about this world. I think it was really smart of them to put me forward because I speak the language of the average person and the average person knows who I am. That way there's a chance people will get to hear my message and that might help somebody. It was worth taking a little bit of flak even if I only helped one person and I think I did OK.

But like I said, Molly wasn't only going to show the good bits!

Halfway through filming the documentary I returned to Britain permanently and moved back into the little farm cottage in Hertfordshire which my brother Max had arranged for me. It was hidden away behind a dairy farm in the middle of nowhere and although it was surrounded by cows and a little isolated, it was more like home than a Paris hotel.

Of course, Molly was also there to capture my 'dark nights of the soul' during those months. I probably revealed more than I should have about my loneliness and low self-esteem, but I was feeling lost. Without the group I didn't know where I was going or what I was for any more. There were so many questions to answer about my future, never mind trying to resolve those about my past. I just felt so miserable but I couldn't understand why. I had always blamed someone or something else for the way I felt and this time it was clear that I had to accept responsibility for my own actions. It says something about how directionless I felt when you realise that I looked to the film for help.

I was bound to attract criticism for being self-indulgent or self-obsessed but then I suppose I often am. At the same time, I have always been motivated by a desire to help others and have learned so much myself from hearing other people's stories. I believed that by sharing my vulnerabilities and letting others see how I was feeling, I might help one person deal with their own problems and realise that they are not alone. We are all looking for confirmation of that.

When I look back at the girl in Molly's film, I can see that she's like a rabbit in the headlights, completely confused about what to do next. It must have seemed foolish to have exposed myself in such a way but there was a part of me that wanted to reveal myself at my lowest ebb and confront whatever reaction came with it.

It was about walking through the fear of humiliation or ridicule and doing it anyway. It was a strange time for me emotionally and I chose to work through it very publicly and very loudly. I sometimes wish I would just take the easy option and do things differently but facing up to fear and doing it anyway has also served me well. I don't suppose I would have achieved half as much if I hadn't.

By the end of the filming, towards the end of 1998, I just wanted to wash my hands of the project. It was all about me and, whatever people might think, I was genuinely bored of the subject! I had enjoyed being with Molly but being on camera constantly was really getting on my nerves. I suppose that was a sign that, slowly, things were improving. By then I was moving into my dream house: an old monastery called St Paul's in Berkshire which I had had gutted and rebuilt.

I left Molly to do the edit. There was no way I was going through all *that* again. Molly had to sift through the hours and hours of material and turn it into a 90 minute film. I decided to let her take it in the direction she wanted because it was her baby. I just asked her to show it to me when she had finished. If there was something completely horrifying to me in the film I hoped she'd show me the grace to remove it but, apart from that, I just had to let it go and wait and see what she came up with.

Throughout this time I was lucky enough to be able to rely on the friendship of George Michael and his partner Kenny Goss. After I left the group I was desperate for somewhere to base myself where I would be protected from the press and where I wouldn't feel alone. I couldn't go home because of my tax year so George and Kenny told me I could stay at their houses in St Tropez and Los Angeles whenever I wanted to. Not only were they generous with their homes but they gave me so much love and support too. I will always be grateful to them for that.

George had been a hero and heartthrob to me since I was a kid buying Wham! records and watching him on *Top of the Pops*. I had dreamed that one day I would be famous and we would meet and fall in love. Well two out of three isn't bad! I first met him at the Capital Music Awards in 1997 and we've been friends ever since. We are both from Watford and are good at keeping each other grounded. We have a lot in common and George has always been a source of wisdom. He kept me calm at the height of the media frenzy and told me to take it easy and not to put too much pressure on myself.

At this time, George had recently lost his mother and was going through his own problems. I think we take refuge with people who we feel some sort of identification with and who we feel safe with. I think he saw me as someone who was very lost and vulnerable and in his humility and compassion he thought, We've all been there. I was really grateful. He was somebody that I had always admired and the fact that he was rooting for me — privately and, whenever he was asked about me, in public — was lovely.

Kenny is adorable. He's a real Texan gentleman. Sometimes when you're just thrown together as we were you get to know each other really quickly. I was pretty miserable at the time so Kenny got to know the core of me instantly. I hope I offered something to him and George too — I think they missed having a female presence around and really responded to me. Kenny and I would go running and play dodge-the-press but most of all we are the perfect shopping partners. He'd guide me around the boutiques in LA helping me choose new outfits. I told him I wanted to look more demure so he'd pick things out and say, 'Now, Geri, what about *this*?' and he was usually right.

It felt like George and Kenny's friendship saved my life.

I have always had a difficult and obsessive relationship with food. As a kid it was used as a comfort and punishment and, because we didn't have much money, treats were rare and closely guarded. I shared with my dad a love of the illicit pleasures of chocolate and ice cream and I always looked forward to our secret trips to the sweet shop. For me, food could be a reward, an anti-depressant or a sedative. My drug of choice was food — sugar.

When I was nineteen and working as a club dancer in Spain, I was hanging out with girls who were very conscious of their body shape and weight. I had never really been worried about these things before. I had always loved my food and I hadn't considered it to be a problem. It wasn't long, though, before I began to look at my own body critically and attempt to control my diet. One evening, after eating at a restaurant and feeling bloated, I went to the toilet, put my fingers down my throat and made myself sick. At first I thought how clever I had been — I'd found a way to eat as much as I liked without getting fat — but at the same time I didn't plan to make a habit of it. It was the beginning of my bulimia.

From that time on, I would always be on one diet or another and a pattern started to develop. I would deny myself food for a while before, eventually, succumbing to temptation and eating until I was sick. The next day I would wake up feeling guilty and disgusted with myself and swear never to do it again and then return to the diet. At the same time, I began to exercise obsessively in an attempt to reduce my weight and work off the calories I had consumed during my latest binge. My eating habits yo-yoed between starvation diets and serious overeating.

Six months before I joined the Spice Girls, when my father died, my dieting developed into anorexia. For a while, I was alarmingly skinny. Throughout my time with the group I battled with bulimia. I would starve myself and get really thin and then find myself alone in a soulless hotel room and, with room service at my fingertips and a mini-bar packed with treats, I would binge, usually until I was sick.

Eating disorders aren't really about food. The issues I had with food were a manifestation of my internal problems and, most importantly, my low self-esteem. I remember telling Molly Dineen one day about how I have never really felt good enough and bingeing would just reinforce these feelings. It was so disgusting that it would confirm my low self-esteem. Even if I wasn't physically acting out bulimia, it came out in different ways. My openness with Molly was an example. I could veer between almost verbally vomiting my feelings one minute and suppressing everything the next.

After the Spice Girls I felt very out of touch with my body. I felt heavy, lethargic and clumsy and my boobs were just so big that I felt blowzy. I don't think this was just a problem with my perception of myself because at the time I left the group I was too big and heavy for a person of my build. I have a small frame and I do not naturally carry weight very well. I felt like I was carrying a suitcase around with me. I was not in good shape for a woman of 25.

As 1998 went on, my eating problems started to calm down because I was under less pressure. I wasn't throwing up or bingeing. That had stopped, and I had actually lost a little bit of weight. The period living with Kenny and George had helped because it gave me some stability. I spent my days with Kenny and we ate proper lunches and dinners at set times. We mostly ate fish and vegetables although I was also cutting down carbohydrates. It was a really difficult adjustment for me. I wasn't used to having any structure whatsoever because I was continually on a diet and though I desperately wanted to eat like a normal person I had dieted for so long that I didn't know how.

A few months after leaving the group, I agreed to speak to *Marie-Claire* magazine about breast cancer awareness and my first post-Spice photo shoot was to be for the magazine's cover in LA. They say the camera puts half a stone on you so I got a trainer and started working out with him just to prepare for this one photo. He told me not to worry and said that a celebrity he trained got ready for her movies by living on water with maple syrup and cayenne pepper for a few days. The cayenne pepper speeds up your metabolism and the maple syrup keeps you sustained. So I decided to give it a try. I lasted a day and I wanted to kill somebody because I was so hungry — the worst-case scenario for me because if I starve myself I run the risk of being catapulted into a frenzy of eating to compensate.

Even though these diets didn't work I persisted with them. My life was dictated by eating or not eating. I would lapse and reward myself with food. I would eat when I was happy, I would eat when I was sad and then I'd go back to a period of not eating. None of it worked but I couldn't stop myself.

·

My mum would come up to the farm cottage every day and my brother lived up the road but I still felt quite isolated there. It was too far from my friends in Watford and too far from London and a bit of a trek from everywhere but, while I waited for my big new house to be finished, it would have to do. My spirits had begun to lift since the initial shock of leaving the band but I still felt lethargic. Exercise usually invigorated me but it wasn't really making an impact. The summer was ending and I found autumn a depressing time. I needed a lift.

Around this time I went to dinner at a posh London restaurant, The Ivy, with George and Kenny, Elton John, Mick Jagger and Jerry Hall and the artist Sam Taylor-Wood who had been nominated for the Turner Prize. I hadn't been out much since I left the group and I felt quite scared because I didn't know Elton well and I didn't know Mick, Jerry or Sam at all. I remember asking Mick how he and Jerry kept their marriage alive and what the secret was of keeping the spark in a relationship. I had no clue that three days later they would announce their divorce. It was a classic case of putting your foot in it and not even realising, well done, Geri!

Sam Taylor-Wood was sitting next to me. She was really quiet but we got talking and after a while she told me that she had been suffering from cancer of the bowel and mentioned how yoga had helped her feel better. I told her that I felt really heavy and sluggish so she suggested I give it a try. She told me about her teacher, a guy called Kisen, and said she would put me in touch with him. A few days later, we had arranged for him to visit me for a lesson.

Life in the farm cottage was chaos. The cottage itself was tiny. It had a little kitchen and front room and two small bedrooms and that was it. There was no room to move with all my belongings crammed in and I had just got my dog Harry from Battersea Dogs' Home. He was a puppy, really hyperactive, and he wasn't house trained. I have to admit that I wasn't the most disciplined pet owner in the world. As a result, he was crapping and peeing everywhere and forever running out into the cowshed, rolling in the hay and the silage then rushing back into the house and making a terrible mess. It was not an ideal situation for my first yoga lesson.

So this was the scene that greeted Kisen when he turned up. He didn't seem to mind but then he's not really your average bloke. He's a Liverpudlian, middle-aged, very lean and a bit hairy. He was wearing a pair of bright yellow high-cut shorts and at one point did a headstand and I got more of a view than I really wanted, but he was very sweet and not at all intimidating. He gave me this little yoga mat to sit on and there and then in this tiny, cramped cottage, I had my first yoga lesson while Harry, who was tethered up, yapped all the way through.

When you start doing yoga, it teaches you that your body is just a body. Nothing more, nothing less. I was very body-conscious and self-conscious but I wasn't in touch with my body, what it can do and how it moves. I was the girl who could never touch her toes and who felt clumsy in the Spice Girls among dancers. I felt very heavy footed and ungraceful.

Kisen started the class and, gradually, my body started to loosen up and I began to feel flexible. As the class continued, I was transported back twenty years to the gym at school. I felt like a child again learning to do a forward roll or a crab or just sitting on my hands and knees. I had stopped being self-conscious about my body and felt at ease. I felt playful again. It didn't matter about the mess or the smell or Harry's noise. I wasn't even bothered by Kisen's yellow shorts any more. It felt so right. After that first lesson I cried my eyes out because I was so happy about the feelings I had rediscovered.

Yoga was perfect for me — exactly what I needed. It helped me feel alive in the present moment, even if that was just for one hour, rather than being focused on tomorrow or next week or next year. Without that help my head was filled with continuous chatter, always thinking about what I should do next or what I should wear or telling myself I wasn't good enough. It was like having a monkey sitting on my shoulder. My head was like a broken television spluttering with interference and with the volume too loud. It wouldn't shut up or give me a moment's peace until I found yoga.

Yoga means a unity of mind and body. I have come to believe that in every cell of our bodies there is an emotional memory and it's stored up. Yoga wrings that emotion out. It allowed me to start letting go of a backlog of pain. But it isn't just about chilling out and being calm. You can do a yoga position that is really feisty and which will enliven your mind. It was just what I needed because it helped me to be centred and, at the same time, woke me up. For the first time in a long time, I felt alive again.

By the time Christmas 1998 came around I was feeling stronger. I was not 100 percent right, I knew that, but I was stronger than when I started working on the documentary with Molly. The finishing touches were being applied to my new house and I was preparing myself to go back out into the world on my own.

Earlier in the year, I had realised that there were lots of things that I wanted to try but that I needed to have one concrete vocation. I decided that it should be my first love — music. When I left the Spice Girls I had told the fans I'd be back and, tentatively, that autumn I had started to write and record. In the New Year of 1999 I was preparing myself to let the world hear what I had come up with. First, though, I had those tough questions to answer from Mr Parkinson.

As it turned out, I needn't have worried. The anticipation was much worse than the real thing and Parky was, as promised, the perfect gentleman. I remember talking very, very fast and babbling away trying to answer his questions about the Spice Girls without upsetting anyone or saying anything I might regret. Slowly I calmed down and by the end I was really enjoying myself.

I was relieved to have survived Britain's biggest interview show without making a fool of myself but now the talking had to stop. I had to start proving myself.

I was about to find out if Geri really could make it on her own.

Look At Me

No matter how difficult I had found life in the Spice Girls, fame had always been my dream, and even if the reality was harder than I'd imagined, I wasn't so ungrateful that I wanted to disappear and leave it all behind. I knew I had something to offer but in that uncertain summer of 1998 I wasn't sure what. The fact that there were so many offers pouring in was reassuring but didn't make it any easier. Where should I start?

I am not the sort of person who can sit still for very long. My dad's death had taught me that time is short and I wanted to keep my mind occupied because it made it easier to deal with the pain of the split. My book, the UN role and Molly's film had kept me busy for a while but I knew that eventually I would have to decide what to do with my career. Music, television and film were all possibilities — I just didn't have a clue which option I should take.

I had a little bit of film experience from making the Spice Girls' movie, *Spiceworld*. I had really enjoyed working on the script with the writer Kim Fuller and even though the whole project was made in a mad hurry, I learnt a lot. When I was acting, I could tell the difference between those times when I was being real and delivering my lines with honesty and when I wasn't. The script wasn't exactly Shakespeare so most of the time I felt like I was pretty crap, but there were about two lines when I thought, Oh, that's quite honest and real. For a first attempt I didn't think I'd done too badly. There were even signs that I might have some talent.

Molly was with me on the day that I had a meeting with the producers of the new James Bond movie. I had always loved the Bond films and the idea of playing an East European assassin or evil femme fatale really appealed to me. I tottered down the street to the audition in high heels and my sharpest black suit, trying out my Russian accent on Molly.

'I can do boxing and kickboxing. So where are ze diamonds, Mr Bond?'

Just as I was about to go in to meet the producers of the movie, Molly threw another of her questions at me. 'Would you go all the way to get the role?' she asked.

'What do you mean?' I said, turning around to face her.

'I mean would you take anything off if that's what they wanted?'

'Oh NO!' I said, outraged. 'I've done all that already!'

I was determined that whatever I did next would give me the chance to explore something new. After four years as Ginger Spice I had done 'sexy' for the time being, so I was looking forward to meeting the Bond producers and part of me really thought I might get the role. A few days later, though, they called me back to let me know that they wouldn't be pursuing the idea any further. I was a little disappointed but had to accept that it just wasn't to be. It looked like I'd have to be my own real-life Bond Girl instead!

Not long after that I was sent a very funny script for a new movie starring Mike Myers in a spoof spy comedy that turned out to be the first Austin Powers film. The character they had in mind was sexy, sassy and larger than life. Remind you of anybody? It was Ginger all over again. I didn't want to repeat myself — I wanted to move on — so I turned the offer down. Even though the movie was a big hit, I have never regretted the decision. What was the point of getting typecast before my film career had even started?

I got sent loads of scripts but none of them really grabbed me. To be honest, I wasn't sure whether I'd be able to recognise a good script when I saw one. I had so little experience in movies and, deep down, I knew I wasn't really ready. Around the same time there were endless stories in the newspapers about film projects I was supposed to be involved in or parts the press said I wanted. One story that kept appearing was that I was after a part in the movie version of *Charlie's Angels*. They said I had discussed the film with the producer Aaron Spelling but was turned down for a part because I was 'too fat'. I had always loved the original show but I had never discussed the movie with a producer and certainly never auditioned. It seems funny now that stories so far from the truth were being printed but at the time they could be hurtful and frustrating. The papers also said I'd met Tom Cruise in Hollywood to discuss my movie career! I wish!

It was all very exciting. The idea of working in the movies, becoming an actress and making it in Hollywood is the stuff that wannabe dreams are made of but I didn't feel confident enough to go for it at the time. The more I thought about it, the more certain I was that my heart belonged to music. I had to admit to myself that deep down a solo career had always been my ultimate intention.

It was scary to own up to the fact that I wanted to try a career as a solo artist. I felt like a school kid going to see my careers officer and telling him I wanted to be a pop star when I grew up. I expected to be told to stop being so silly and think about a proper job. In the Spice Girls I had four other people to help me and to some extent, I could hide. By admitting I wanted to go solo, I was saying that I thought I could make it on my own. I knew that most people — or at least those 'experts' who wrote me off in the newspapers — thought the idea was a joke. As far as they were concerned, I couldn't sing, couldn't dance and was too fat. It took a lot of strength not to believe them.

First, I needed a team to give me the confidence to take on the task and make it happen. Matthew Freud and his company had done a fantastic job running my PR since I left the group and he told me in New York that autumn that I had to really focus if my music career was going to work out. It was time to get a manager and, through a friend of a friend, I was introduced to Lisa Anderson. Lisa is amazing. She's a pioneer who's made a hugely successful career in a very male-dominated industry and is a fantastic mix of a powerful, sharp, intelligent businesswoman and a glamorous, loving mother with red lipstick and two enormous poodles. Although she was already very busy running the Brits as well as her young family, I really wanted to work with her and managed to persuade her to take me on.

The next thing I had to do was get myself a record contract. When I was a Spice Girl I had been on Virgin, which is part of EMI, but I thought it wouldn't be right to stay there and share a label with the girls. Your label is your team and I don't think it would have been fair to expect that team to divide their loyalties between the girls and a solo ex-member. At the same time, I didn't really want to leave the company because they had shown me such loyalty and support. I felt at home there and I think they were very grateful for the part I had played in the Spice Girls. After all, we had earned EMI a lot of money.

One of the bosses of the company at the time was a guy called Ken Berry. Ken had known me as a young pup when I started out with the group and he had always shown me an enormous amount of faith and respect. Ken called me one day and said he wanted to give me a chance and had an idea how it could be done. Why not sign for Chrysalis — a subsidiary of EMI — so that I could remain within the family without treading on the girls' toes? It was the perfect solution and I was very happy to agree. Nobody really knew how it would work out — there were no guarantees that Geri Halliwell would be as successful as Ginger Spice — but I was so grateful that I was being given the chance to find out.

The person responsible for looking after me at Chrysalis was an A&R guy called Chris Briggs. As soon as I met him I could tell that I would get the right sort of attention and that he understood where I was coming from. It helped that he looked after the career of another artist who had been a member of a leading group and then left — Robbie Williams. It was good to know he'd had that sort of experience and I felt safe with him. So Chris had Robbie and now he had me.

You couldn't meet a more laid back A&R man than Chris. He's very warm and sweet and he's not controlling. It was really important to me that he would give an opinion without trying to force it on me. I had no real idea what I wanted to do musically but I knew I had to grow and discover for myself. I didn't want to be told I should be doing one style or another or that I had to use a particular producer just because that was what the record company demanded. I wanted to find my own voice and I think Chris thought I'd earned the right to a little grace, so he gave me some room to do my own thing.

It might seem like a reasonable bet for a record company to give someone like me a chance, given my experience and my high profile, but at the time it seemed like absolutely everybody else thought I couldn't do it. The papers were full of bitchy comments about my abilities and unfavourable comparisons with the other girls. Ginger Spice had worked because she was a brash character in a pop gang but on her own and without the war paint? Forget it! It felt like a lot of people were waiting to see me fall flat on my face.

I have to admit that I may not have been acting from the healthiest motivation. A big part of me just wanted to show the world that I could do it and I think the fact that everyone said I couldn't sing or dance worked like reverse psychology for me. The more people doubted me, the more determined I was to show them that I could make it on my own. It comes back to proving that 'they' are wrong, but who are 'they' really? 'They' usually turn out to be self-appointed experts with column inches to fill. At the same time, I realised that the most important person I had to prove it to was myself because, inside, I had the same doubts as everybody else:

Can I sing? Can I dance? Can I carry this on my own?

The bottom line is that I was really lacking in confidence as a singer. I didn't come from a trained background and I knew I was no Mariah or Whitney. On the other hand, I had been singing since I was a little girl and had gained fantastic experience during my four years with the Spice Girls. Even so, I decided I needed to get some help.

I arranged to meet my voice coach Russell in the same west London studios where I had auditioned for the Spice Girls. I remember this huge Viking of a man who looked like an opera singer (which, it turned out, he was) coming into the studios to put me through my paces. Despite his overpowering appearance he was very sweet and taught me so much. He explained that the vocal chords are like any other muscles in the body, they need stretching and working out. As he got me used to practising scales and learning how to breathe I could feel my confidence starting to build. I was like a sportsman working with a coach, learning skills and getting match fit. Even if I would never be a great diva, with Russell's help I had a good chance of making it as a solo pop star.

The next step was giving myself a test run in the recording studio. I had worked with the Absolute production team — Paul Watson and Andy Watkins — since the early days of the Spice Girls. They had collaborated with the girls and myself on Spice classics like 'Say You'll Be There' and 'Who Do You Think You Are?' and I felt very comfortable with them. I knew they believed I had the talent to make it because they had seen me deliver the goods in the past. I wanted to write and record my solo album with them.

In the car on the way down to their recording studio in south London in the afternoon after that first yoga class, I was feeling high and exhilarated. The yoga had felt like a breakthrough and I was ready to channel all that energy into my first solo recording. George had always told me to take my time when it came to my solo career, reassuring me that 'The world will wait for you, Geri, so if you do decide to put a record out, make sure it's good.' As part of that process he suggested I try singing a song called 'Broken Heart' that a friend of his had written. So 'Broken Heart' was the song I took into the studio that afternoon. Paul and Andy were very welcoming and supportive but it was nerve-wracking new territory for me. I felt embarrassed and exposed going into the little booth to sing and the first few times I opened my mouth to sing I sounded terrible. I was so nervous and uptight but Paul and Andy are past masters at making me relax.

'Shit! Is this getting any better?' I said as another run-through collapsed in failure.

'Keep going, Geri,' Andy said. 'You'll get there in the end.'

Gradually, as the session progressed, I started to loosen up and eventually I finished the song and it sounded OK. I started to believe that I could do it. It had been a good day.

For me, being a solo artist is not just about singing, it's also about performance and songwriting. I played an active role in writing Spice Girls material and enjoyed coming up with hooks or little melody lines but the most fulfilling part had always been the lyrics. So that autumn, I began to write.

I had plenty of material to draw on because I had so much on my mind — leaving the group, losing my father — and songwriting was a fantastic way of working through those feelings and expressing myself.

Soon I was back in the studio showing my lyrics and melody ideas to the Absolute boys and we started to work out how they could be turned into songs. It was difficult because the lyrics were so personal but I had grown really close to Paul and Andy over the years. With anyone else I would have been worried that they'd laugh at me or tell me my words were crap but I felt safe with them. The best thing was the way they embraced all my mad ideas. Andy and I would lie on the floor with a pad of paper full of lyrics while Paul played piano and tried to come up with melody ideas. I'd say 'I want a Spanish vibe on this song' or 'I want this to sound like some mad sixties Shirley Bassey show stopper!' and they'd try to come up with a way of using my idea. It was a real collaboration and I got a kick out of it. I loved it in the studio because I lost all sense of time, forgot my worries and just focused on the songs and the creative process. It was perfect escapism.

As usual, I was in a real hurry to make progress. I didn't want to let anybody hear the songs until they were almost finished, so nobody had the chance to voice an opinion except the boys and me. By Christmas of 1998, we had thirteen songs — more than enough for an album. Eventually Paul and Andy would play the music to their girlfriends and I'd play it to some close friends. Only then would I let Chris Briggs have a listen. We kept it to a very small number of people at first but whenever anyone did hear some of the music they were impressed and I started to get really excited about showing the world what I'd achieved.

By the time I was on *Parkinson* in the New Year of 1999 I knew what I had but I was still wary about talking it up too much. I told Parky about my album but pointed out that success was not guaranteed. I was not being modest, that was how I felt. I was proud but nervous. It was time to find out if the world still loved me.

That January I was still going through my mourning period. The way I dressed and presented myself was very telling. I was wearing black and had my hair up in a sensible, mature style, reacting against my Ginger past. I wanted to look anonymous and part of me still wanted to hide.

When spring came, I started to feel alive again. I seem to reflect the seasons — from October to February I almost hibernate, hide in bed in a little cocoon and wait for spring because I know that then I'll feel ready to blossom again. So I started coming out of myself more. I felt a bit more confident and started to take an interest in going shopping. I had forgotten what I liked when it came to clothes so I started experimenting and enjoying the idea of being a little bit more adventurous. I bought a pair of Joseph trousers and a pair of flat shoes and it felt fantastic. I had been wearing heels since I was seventeen because the extra height seemed to lift me up and elongated me, making me feel less fat. It was exciting to come down a few inches in a pair of normal shoes.

St Paul's, my big new house in the country was finally ready too. The building, an old monastery, was set in eighteen acres of grounds and surrounded by a high brick wall and had been completely gutted and renovated. I had been doing a lot of shopping with my friend Linda Page, an interior designer and architect, and had found all the fixtures and fittings I needed to make my dream house a reality. It felt really grown up going to antique shops with Linda to find stuff to deck the house out with. I wanted the place to look grand and I admit that some of the furniture was a bit over the top and Elton John with lots of gold trim and ornate carving. But it was a wonderful feeling to walk through the doors when it was finished and know that this was home. I had been on the move ever since I left home when I was sixteen. Maybe this was somewhere I could put down some roots at last.

I always think of St Paul's as my *Gone With the Wind* house. I had dreamed ever since childhood of owning one like it. There is an enormous staircase in the entrance hall that was made for Scarlett O'Hara to sweep down and a grand dining room in red with a huge table, eighteen chairs and a print of 'The Last Supper' hanging on the wall. In all there are seventeen rooms, including seven bedrooms. One of these bedrooms is 'Dad's Room' and I know he would have been very proud that his daughter should end up in such a grand place. I thought that it would be the perfect place to hide away and find some privacy because it was so isolated — the only other people around were the nuns who lived in the convent next door.

Finishing the house and my record coming together helped me to feel more positive — completing projects and building things gives you self-esteem. At the same time, I started to feel a bit prettier and decided I was ready to ditch the mature look and act my age! I was only twenty-six and while I didn't want to look like Ginger any more I did want to feel attractive.

It's amazing the difference a haircut can make and early in 1999 I went to see my hairdresser Ken to work on a new look. I told him I wanted to lose the sensible hair and find something that was both fun and tasteful — time to lighten up. Ken suggested I give blonde extensions a try and I felt such a sense of relief when I saw myself in the mirror that day. Gone was the UN ambassador, dowdy look — I felt like a girl again! It was wonderful to feel feminine and pretty.

My self-esteem has always been connected to my weight. Travel and overwork were constant triggers for my bulimia and bingeing when I was in the Spice Girls and my more stable life had helped me lose a little weight. I had also found a new diet that had started to pay off. The Dr Atkins diet involves cutting down on carbohydrates like potatoes and pasta because when there are no carbs to burn the body burns fat. I didn't follow it to the letter but I was aware of the principle and started limiting the carbs I ate. The results started to come fairly quickly.

The Capital Radio Awards in March 1999 were like a coming-out party for me. I had a new look to show off and I was stepping back into the celebrity limelight. I was feeling nervous about the occasion so it was a relief to have George by my side. He was picking up an award and it helped to know that he would be deflecting some of the attention. All I wanted was to get through the occasion and let people know that Geri wasn't all sober suits and serious subjects. My new look announced that I was back and in a different frame of mind. I looked different on the outside because I was feeling better on the inside. It was partly a conscious move but it was also an expression of natural changes that had been taking place in my life.

I felt like I had my bullets in my bag and I was ready to go out and show the world what I could do. I had decided that the first single should be a song called 'Look At Me', which was a bold choice and a real statement of intent. I wanted to tell the world that I was back and this seemed the best way to do it. Most of all I wanted it to go to Number One and prepared myself for a gruelling round-the-world promotional tour aimed at achieving exactly that. The race was on and I was all fired up again.

'Look At Me' was my choice. I didn't think that I could be shy about my comeback and thought it was a good idea to return with a song that people would either love or hate but couldn't be indifferent to. 'Look At Me' was in your face and full of attitude and that seemed like the right message to send. At the same time, the song appealed to me because it had an ironic sense of humour which was aimed at myself as much as anything. I was aware that I had an image as someone pushy who wanted to be the centre of attention all the time, so the title was intended to show a bit of humour and self-awareness. I thought the song was fun and very playful. I was sick of sensible Geri and wanted to move on and it was the perfect vehicle.

I rarely let the record company decide what songs I should release as singles. I prefer to rely on the advice of the most honest and intuitive audience available — kids. One day, when he was over for a visit with his mum, I put my little nephew Alistair into the back of my car and took him out for a spin. He might have thought this was just a fun trip to the shops but I had other ideas. After a few minutes I put a copy of 'Look At Me' in the car stereo and watched how he reacted. Would he bounce up and down? Would he nod his head in time with the music? Would he just stare out of the window or, worst of all, put his hands over his ears and scream? It was a relief when his head started bobbing and his legs got going. When that happens you know you've got something catchy going on. 'Look At Me' it was.

The song had a big Shirley Bassey and sixties influence mixed in with a hard-edged dance feel. I hadn't gone with the most commercial single in the world — it's not really a nice and pleasant pop song. We came up with a very dramatic moment in the middle of the song where the whole thing breaks down into this weird section with lots of freaky horns and wailing backing singers and when we sent it over to America they just couldn't handle it. They were like, 'What the hell is this? We can't have this on radio! Oh my God, this is not working for us!' So we had to cut the middle part out for the Americans because it was too much for them to bear! 'Look At Me' got those kinds of reactions but this wasn't a time for half-measures and that's why I chose it. I was drawn to the risk.

I wanted to make a video that could contain all the ideas and influences that I had been writing down and soaking up for months. I brought in the director Vaughan Arnell, who I knew from the Spice Girls, and told him that I wanted to do something influenced by the Audrey Hepburn movies I'd been watching and films like *La Dolce Vita*. 'Look At Me' was about all the different masks we wear and the different roles women play. It was a chance to indulge my Hollywood fantasies. I appeared as the virgin bride, the vamp, the bitch and the nun and it was all shot in black and white and set in Prague. Not your average pop video.

For the freaky middle section we had an old horse-drawn hearse carrying a coffin to the cemetery. The coffin was draped in a Union Jack with a wreath spelling out 'GINGER' on the side. That was my dark sense of humour — Ginger is Dead. I remember lying in the coffin in the freezing cold in Prague with long red tresses and red ballet shoes. The idea was to look like the Pre-Raphaelite beauties I'd seen in paintings like 'Flaming June' or 'Ophelia'. It wasn't supposed to be too serious but I did want the video to make the point that I had moved on. And now, if Ginger was finally dead, it seemed only sensible — and hygienic — to bury her. Ginger went out in the way she would have liked, with a funeral on *Top of the Pops*.

It was an exciting moment for me because the interest and expectation around the record was enormous. I could tell that I had everyone's attention and that people were genuinely interested in what I was going to come up with, even if most of them expected it to be a crock of shit. When we played the song to different DJs before its official release the feedback was good. I think there was a real sense of surprise because expectations were so low that anything better than terrible was going to be a bit of a triumph. Aside from those who just wanted to be negative, I think people in general were willing to give me the benefit of the doubt. I had taken a gamble leaving the Spice Girls when I did and I was about to find out if I'd made a big mistake or if I could make it by myself. There was no doubt about the standard I had set myself — a Number One record. Nothing less would do.

When I was growing up, getting a Top Ten hit counted as a big success. In the seventies and eighties, songs would climb their way gradually up the pop charts before finally reaching Number One. It was very rare for a song to enter the charts at the top. In the last ten years all that's changed. These days the charts are fast and furious — you go in at Number One and then you're out. Singles rarely stay at the top much longer than a week and if a single misses out on the Number One slot in the first week, it rarely makes it afterwards. It's like a test-your-strength machine at the fairground — you give it your best shot and you either hit the bell or you don't. And having been in a group like the Spice Girls — I had seven Number Ones with them, all of which went straight in at the top — the pressure was enormous.

Whether a single will make it can depend a lot on what else is being released at the same time. When you choose the week of release it's natural to check out the competition and figure out who you are up against. If you're sensible, you avoid the bigger acts and choose a quiet week but that isn't my style. I believed in the single and video so much that I was willing to take a risk. I love a gamble and the higher the stakes, the greater the thrill, so I decided to release the single the same week as Boyzone released their new song 'You Needed Me'. Boyzone were at the height of their success at the time and had scored their fifth Number One single two months before. All five of their Number Ones had gone straight in at the top. It was like playing Russian roulette with my career — all or nothing.

Of course, I was only one part of the team responsible for making the dream a reality. I needed to make sure that the people working on my record would get out there and fight for it and feel it as personally as I did. The radio girl who tried to get the record airplay had to love my record if the DJ was going to play it and the man who distributed the single to Woolworths had to fight my corner to get it in the shops so that people could buy it.

I remember sitting down with the staff at the record company and giving them a little speech:

'I love pop music and I'm proud of what I did in the Spice Girls,' I said, looking around the room making eye contact with my new team. 'I hate it when people leave bands and say they never liked the music. So I will never trash the Spice Girls! They gave me so much and I am not going to go around saying that they are uncool or rubbish. A good example of that was Bros. I remember they criticised the group's music. You won't be hearing that from me.'

I was about to move on to my next point about how much I believed in the record when I sensed I might be losing the audience a little. Some of them seemed to be suppressing giggles and others were looking a bit uncomfortable. Then I realised why. As I looked down the room I saw Craig, the non-blond one from Bros, sitting there looking a bit awkward. *Oh dear*. He worked for the record company and he was going to be on my team. Luckily, Craig took it well. 'Don't worry,' he said. 'No offence.' So I had to try and continue the speech with my foot in my mouth. It wasn't the best start but by the time 'Look At Me' was released they were all as fired up and excited as I was.

In April 1999 my comeback was launched on the world — literally. A whistle-stop promotional tour had been planned which would take me around the world in eight days. I was to start in Rio then go to New York, Canada, Japan, Australia and Milan. Finally, I'd go back to London to Radio One and present DJ Zoe Ball with a copy of the single to play on her Breakfast Show. As if that wasn't enough, I decided to combine the trip with the start of filming for a new venture I had taken on, a TV show called *Geri's World Walkabout*.

Paul Jackson, who was at the BBC at the time, had approached me in 1998 to see if I'd be interested in presenting a show. I didn't want to do TV full time but I said I was interested in one-off projects if I felt they were right for me. So I sat down with Paul and a director called David Green one day and bounced ideas around. I mentioned that it would be really interesting to ask the same questions about life of a kid from India and a kid from Los Angeles and see if they came up with similar answers. What do they believe in? What is their faith and how do they get by in life?

We used this as the starting point for the programme and developed it from there. I had been to many different countries in the last few years but had rarely seen more than brief glimpses of reality through the tinted windows of limousines or from the safety of my hotel suite. I wanted to meet inspirational and unusual people from all over the world and give them a chance to tell me their stories and perhaps learn something about the real world that seemed to be passing me by. So David Green set his programme team to work. They came back to me with about 50 stories from around the world. I spent a few days at St Paul's, sitting at my kitchen table working through them, and picked the ones that I found most interesting. As usual, I was packing a hell of a lot in but I was looking forward to stepping outside the comfort zone of my normal life and getting a reality check. And that was exactly what I got.

The first leg of the whistle-stop tour was Rio de Janeiro, Brazil, where the weather was beautiful and the sea and beaches very tempting. It would have been lovely to have just relaxed and enjoyed myself but I had work to do. The *Walkabout* team had scheduled four interviews in one day. The first was with a guitar-playing Catholic priest called Father Zeca who had a record deal with EMI. It was interesting because he was quite young and good-looking and I had a pretty good idea that the girls who went to his services might have been there for non-religious reasons! They were fans of the priest more than worshippers and got God as a kind of extra on top of seeing their heartthrob. So he sang a song on his acoustic guitar and then we talked.

This was the first television interview I had ever done so I was obviously just finding my feet. In a way this gave me an advantage because I brought a beginner's cheek to the process. I wasn't afraid to break the rules and ask the questions that everyone thinks about but most interviewers are too afraid or too polite to ask. I asked him if it was difficult living without sex, especially when he was surrounded by a beautiful teenage congregation. He seemed a little uncomfortable with the question but implied that when he was younger he'd been there and done that. I was starting to have fun with this and my next question was a bit near to the knuckle, even by my standards:

'It's commendable that you've given up sex for religion but do you still do those natural things that men do without women? Are you allowed to do that or not?'

Father Zeca looked a little uncomfortable but, to his credit, he managed an answer. 'No... No,' he said. 'I channel all of that into my services.'

No wonder his congregations were so full of young women, I thought, which brought me on to my next question.

'We are in a world where AIDS is rife. What do you say to a girl who comes to you for advice about contraception?'

This time I'd gone too far. No matter how funky this particular padre was, he wasn't going to go against the Catholic Church's view that using contraception was a sin. He just smiled, his previously fantastic English deserting him.

'It's too difficult for me to talk about in English. Anyway.'

And it was time for another song.

From there on, the Rio trip was unrelenting. In a single day I interviewed a young woman who had contracted AIDS from an infected partner during her first sexual encounter and talked to street children who lived with the risk of police violence. The final interview was with an incredible boy called Reginaldo who was the 'Brazilian Billy Elliot'. He was a ballet dancer living in a shanty town in the Brazilian slums who'd won a scholarship to the Bolshoi Ballet in Russia. It was amazing! It was such an eye-opener and a humbling experience to see where he lived. He and his family shared a tiny little hut with hardly any furniture and only the most basic facilities, a world away from the one I was used to and the posh hotel I was staying in just a few miles away. But it was also great fun to meet Reginaldo and all the little kids who swarmed around me when I arrived at his house. I loved his story. Anything is possible in life — it's only our minds that close off possibilities and Reginaldo was living proof of that. He had found a way to get himself out of his situation and grabbed the opportunity with both hands. People have always said that I am ambitious and driven as if they are dirty words but I think Reginaldo's story shows what a bit of drive and ambition can do. It can take you from the slums of Rio to the Bolshoi Ballet.

I remember watching Reginaldo doing his ballet steps dressed all in white in the middle of this slum and wondering where he'd got the courage to go against the macho culture that surrounded him. I didn't know if he was an Arthur or a Martha and I have to admit I was curious.

I told the interpreter that I wanted to know whether Reginaldo had a girlfriend or a boyfriend. The interpreter asked him something but even with my non-existent Portuguese I could tell that whatever question he'd asked it wasn't that one!

'You didn't translate the whole thing!' I said to the interpreter on camera. He just acted like he didn't understand — which was strange behaviour for an interpreter if you think about it — but I suppose it was for the best that it went over Reginaldo's head.

After doing the interviews for *Walkabout* and the promotional work in Rio we flew to New York. I was with my PA, Victoria, a girl from the record company and a photographer I have worked with since Spice Girl days called Dean Freeman, whose photos are in this book. It was just the start of the trip but we were already relying on adrenalin to carry us through. I felt like I was on a mission and was enjoying being back in the madness of it all. I remember scurrying around in my little flat shoes finding it all very exciting again and the others fed off that. Excitement is contagious.

The fuss that surrounded me during the trip seemed ridiculous at times. In New York we were on our way to a press conference and there was a huge crowd waiting outside. I had a security man called Lou Palumbo. He is a brilliant bodyguard, a real veteran, but the whole drama around me seemed so stupid and funny. It started to rain, really piss down, and I heard Lou talking into his walky-talky to other security staff. He sounded so worried and I remember him saying, 'We have a situation. There is precipitation on the principal,' and Victoria, Dean and I just cracked up in a fit of giggles.

The TV and promo tour was a real eye-opener. Seeing the poverty in Rio did make me put my own troubles in perspective. There's me moaning about my stupid eating disorders or my weight when someone else is really on the breadline or in a life and death situation. It compelled me to try and be more positive and be really, really grateful. I never want to undermine addictions and illnesses because they are all life threatening and everybody has worries, but sometimes, I realised, I needed a kick up the arse and some of those stories did that.

The problem is that those feelings can never really last. You can compare it to when you go on holiday and feel peaceful watching the sunset over the sea and want to hold on to that feeling when you get back to your life. But sure enough, you get consumed and caught up in your everyday dramas and decisions and minor worries all over again. Sunsets and other people's miseries become a distant memory once you get back to your own life. For me, trivial though it was in comparison, I had Boyzone to worry about.

We had hired a private jet for the tour and after New York we flew to Canada then onto the really long flight to Japan. We would sleep on the jet, get off, do the meet and greets, show the video, do the press conference, get back on the plane and sleep again. Then it was Australia, where we stayed for seven hours before Milan and another press conference. When I was interviewed I was quite honest about my feelings about my new single — I was nervous as hell. From Milan it was back home to London to deliver the record to Radio One and then the countdown would really begin.

Zoe Ball took delivery of the single and kicked off the last month of 'Look At Me' promotion between the first airplay and the week of release. I was pleased that reactions were generally good but it seemed to me I wasn't hearing the song on the radio enough. It was not quite cool enough for Radio One but a bit obscure for Capital so I don't think the radio people knew where to place it. As the time approached it was clear it was going to be a close-run thing.

The situation was complicated by the fact that Boyzone had released two versions of their CD single *and* they had made theirs cheaper. Right at the start we discussed whether we should do something similar but everybody, myself included, decided to keep it simple and release one version at the standard price. The cost of that decision became clear as the week went on. Boyzone's army of fans went out and bought both versions of their single so even though they were buying the same song twice, it counted as two sales. My fans only had one CD to buy and, even though there were more transactions over the counter involving my record, the competition was creeping ahead.

When the Sunday came I was at home at St Paul's, pacing the seventeen rooms, unable to settle down or think straight. The promotion had been a whirlwind, picking me up and taking me around the world, but now it had stopped, dropping me here in my enormous house. Now there was only silence and waiting.

At lunchtime the phone rang. I rushed to pick it up and immediately recognised Lisa's voice on the end of the line. 'I'm sorry,' she said and I knew I had failed. In the end it was only a matter of a few hundred records. 'You Needed Me' by Boyzone was straight in at Number One. 'Look At Me' by Geri Halliwell was Number Two.

I had enjoyed returning to the fray and even got a kick out of the insane promotion schedule. I had been happy to go through all the radio interviews and record-shop signings and, all in all, the chase for the top had been a buzz. But now all of my hard work and sense of hope and anticipation had fallen flat. I had known it would be difficult but every other time I'd gone out there to get something I had succeeded and deep down, I thought that I would do it again. The disappointment was dreadful — it felt almost physical.

Do you remember how it used to be on the BBC at midnight when the programmes would end — shut down. It felt a bit like that. I felt empty. Had I lost the plot? Maybe I couldn't pick singles or write good pop songs any more and maybe, after all my success down the years, I was getting too big for my boots. After all, we only gamble because we think we are so naturally lucky that we just can't lose. Maybe my luck had run out.

My next reaction was to go into denial and try and kid myself that everything was fine and that Number Two was a fantastic achievement. It didn't work. Number One had always been the prize and I hadn't won it. I also felt furious — with myself as much as anybody — for making the mistake with the formats and the price. It felt like I'd lost because of a cock-up more than anything else.

My dream was that 'Look At Me' was going to blow the roof off but now I didn't know where its relative failure left me. There was the chance that I had made a massive mistake walking out on the biggest band in Britain and that I was on my way to the Where Are They Now? file. Did my fans still love me or had I lost them when I walked out of the Spice Girls and waved goodbye to Ginger Spice? I had no way of knowing but the early signs didn't look too good. Would I even have a career in six months?

The gambler in me had been compelled to play for the highest stakes by taking on a huge and established chart group like Boyzone at the height of their popularity. I had to question the wisdom of my decision but I realised that I wasn't always driven by the most practical or sensible considerations. I was also worried that my mistake with the single was about to be overshadowed by an even greater error of judgement — the decision to allow Molly Dineen to film me the previous summer.

Geri: The Movie was about to arrive in prime time.

Just One Girl

I'm not sure what I was expecting but I certainly didn't like what I saw. An image of myself in a blue and white bikini, squinting into the sunlight, appeared on the TV monitor in front of me. I listened as the words tumbled out of my mouth, my emotions laid bare in a non-stop stream of consciousness. I watched as I slapped on the suntan cream, hot and bothered on the roof terrace at the Crillon Hotel, Paris. I completely cringed at myself as I sat beside Molly watching the final cut of the programme.

On 5th May 1999, Channel 4 devoted an hour and a half to a documentary about a lonely, confused young woman baring her soul about life, death, low self-esteem and isolation. It sounds fairly typical for a weeknight on Channel 4 but the viewing figures were anything but — 4.5 million viewers tuned in on a Wednesday night and Channel 4 liked it so much they showed it all over again a month later. Molly Dineen's documentary, *Geri,* was a big hit.

I had realised pretty early on in the filming that I wasn't in the best place to make a documentary but by then it was too late and when filming was finished I couldn't exactly stamp my feet and demand the footage back. I had made a commitment and I had to see it through to the bitter end.

Occasionally I would go into the edit suite where Molly was putting the film together. She would show me little bits — me opening my heart in the back of the car or getting emotional at home in the cottage — but I found it hard to see it objectively. How could I tell whether it was good or not? After all, I was up there on the screen and my judgement was clouded by my embarrassment and fear. I was more focused on trying to work out whether the film would completely destroy my career or help people understand where I was coming from. In the end I just had to put my faith in the fact that Molly was a nice person. She was a journalist with a point of view but I trusted her enough to believe that she wasn't going to annihilate me and portray me in a bad light. So I let her get on with it.

One day in the spring of 1999 Molly called to say she had a final version for me to come in and watch. I could feel butterflies in my stomach as I made my way to the edit suite that afternoon. I kept telling myself it would be OK — after all, how bad could it really be? I hadn't done anything terrible or said anything I didn't mean. Had I? I arrived to find Molly waiting. If she was nervous about my reaction she wasn't showing it. She just smiled and gave me a cup of tea.

'Are you ready, Geri?' she asked.

This was the moment of the truth. I was about to find out if my instincts were right about Molly and the whole project or if I had made a horrendous mistake. Molly had been there with her camera during a period of darkness in my life — probably the worst emotional place I had been through in all my years on this planet — and I was about to relive it.

'OK,' I said, bracing myself. 'Let's do it.'

Right from the start I was cringing, squirming in my seat as I watched myself. Oh my God, do I talk like that? Oh my God, is that really how fat I look? Surely I don't walk like *that*? If someone plays your voice back that's enough to irritate you but I was watching myself from every imaginable angle and it was unbearable. Every mannerism or characteristic seemed to be magnified and exaggerated in an unpleasant way. It was like, Is this who I am? Is this what I am really like? Molly showed me coming out of the loo, washing my hair and biting my nails. I was happy, sad, manic and subdued and I talked and talked and talked.

I particularly hated those sequences on the sun terrace at the Crillon Hotel in Paris where I had spent part of my tax year away. I came across like a bumbling idiot, babbling about my life to anyone who would listen. I hated the way I sounded and I hated the way I looked. Some of those parts were just too painful to watch and there were moments where I said to Molly, 'Please, no, this is horrifying.'

There is a part in the documentary where Molly asks me why I left the Spice Girls. I gave an answer I regret giving so much that I'm not even going to repeat it here. As I watched it back that day I felt very uneasy about leaving it in. Almost a year had passed since I'd said it and I wasn't sure I felt so clear about it any more. It seemed to me it was really there for the titillation factor so I asked Molly to cut it from the film. I hoped she'd see that it was difficult for me to include something so direct but she was adamant — it had to be addressed and the comment had to stay. I could have shouted and screamed about it but I decided, reluctantly, to just let it pass. I had to respect Molly by allowing her to make her programme. Otherwise, I could have employed somebody to do exactly what I chose, which might have made me look good but would have been pretty boring for the viewers.

In the end, Molly has an angle like anyone else. The film couldn't be a one hundred percent accurate reflection of the reality of my life but it was Molly's selection of the bits she thought were the most interesting or revealing. I didn't come across as a nasty or unpleasant person in the film. I just seemed lost and alone because that was how I was at the time. The most difficult thing was going to be living with the consequences once the programme was broadcast. I knew I wanted the programme to help me to eradicate my Ginger image on national TV but I didn't know what I was putting in her place.

What the hell would people think when they saw it? Millions of viewers were about to sit in the comfort of their living rooms watching me fall apart. What would they think of me? Would they hate me? Would they laugh at me?

On the night itself I wanted to run a million miles from it but I only made it as far as Germany where I was doing promo work. I had taken my mum along to distract me and I was pretty grateful that they couldn't get Channel 4 in Frankfurt! I was so terrified about the way people might react that I just pretended it wasn't happening and got on with my job. But I couldn't hide for ever. I had to return home and face the music.

In the end I was relieved because the overwhelming reaction I received back in Britain was sympathy. I was right to be concerned that people would think I appeared sad and pathetic because some did think that but most people just wanted to comfort me. When people saw me on the street after that they would come up to me, put their hand on my arm and look at me intently and say:

'Are you alright?'

'Yes. I'm fine,' I'd answer, smiling.

'Are you *sure*?'

'I'm sure.'

Well, certainly the whole Ginger illusion thing had been completely shattered. Suddenly people realised that I was a real person with real feelings who gets lonely and unhappy just like they do. A lot of people who might have been afraid of me before wanted to be my friend after that. It felt very nice but it was hard to take as well. I felt a little embarrassed because now I was this needy chick and everybody knew about it. It was also strange because the documentary was already so out of date. That phase of my life seemed a distant memory because so much had happened in the time since it was filmed.

Sometimes the sympathy would come out as pity. Some people saw me as a sad and lost figure and I had exposed myself to ridicule by admitting to feeling lonely or unhappy. On the other hand, many people came up to me and said, 'You know what, Geri? I feel the same.' People still come up to me today and thank me for saying that I felt lonely and cried at the weekends because I had nothing to take the place of work. Half the population of Britain has probably felt the same way at some time in their lives. I think I reminded people that they are not alone.

When the reaction wasn't sympathy or pity it was something close to anger. I think many people looked at me and thought, Who do you think you are? They wanted to shake me and tell me to stop whingeing and appreciate how lucky I was. People who can't pay their rent or are struggling to pay their electricity bill would kill to have what I had. They looked upon me as a spoilt little girl with too much money, too much fame and too much time. So I can understand why people said, 'What the hell has she got to whinge about?' It was fair comment but at the same time it doesn't matter who you are or how famous you are, everybody's got pain.

Molly's film blew away the myth that celebrity brings happiness. Here was this little girl rattling around in her huge house trying to realise dreams that were obviously not filling her up, still very lonely and unhappy, despite worldwide success and fame and money. The whole thing questions our values because it makes you think about whether material things bring happiness. I was living proof that it wasn't so. I had believed that if I got rich and famous, I would be really happy because the television told me I would. I lived that dream and it turned out to be a lie.

I look back on my decision to take part in that documentary now and wonder what on earth I was thinking. In many ways it was unwise and I didn't really think it through or fully realise its consequences. But in the end, I'm proud of the film because it's honest. I can't take the credit for that because Molly had the skill to make me forget the camera was there and open my heart and soul to her as a human being rather than a journalist. I don't think the programme really did my public image or my career too much harm either. In the eighties stars like Michael Jackson or Prince had an air of mystery about them and they came across as untouchable and inaccessible but in the 21st century that no longer works — people want aspirational figures who are also accessible.

Even during the making of the documentary I realised that I couldn't give people a one-dimensional character any more because that's not what they wanted. The public want to see you, feel you and touch you enough to know you are real. That's exactly what they got! And as for Ginger, she was publicly demolished with a sledgehammer!

There wasn't time for me to sit around and worry about the documentary or dwell on my disappointment about 'Look At Me' for long. I had a new round of promotional work to get on with to support the release of my first solo album *Schizophonic* and was due to give my first live performance as a solo artist at the G.A.Y club night at the London Astoria. I knew the Astoria well. As I arrived there that night, I was transported back to my late teens when I was a nightclub dancer there, shaking my stuff on the podium on a Saturday night. I was the complete wannabe in those days, dreaming I was the new Madonna or any kind of star at all. I also thought about one of the Spice Girls' earliest performances when we played G.A.Y to promote 'Wannabe'. It had felt amazing to start making my dreams a reality that night but this was even better. I was back, on my own and with George Michael by my side. Not a bad result all round.

The gay audience have always been supportive of me. There was a really camp side to the Spice Girls — you might have noticed — and Ginger was in the tradition of strong, larger-than-life women who appeal to gay men. I think they respond to my combination of glamour and humour and enjoy the very female side of me that loves high heels, hotpants and lipstick as well as that part of me that is kind of ballsy. They also respond to my honesty about my weaknesses. Celebrating your sexuality is a brave and not very British thing to do and showing your vulnerability is not exactly stiff upper lip either. I felt safe there and thought they would probably support me even if I forgot the words or fell over on my backside.

I was very nervous that night because it was a big deal for me to try to carry a performance on my own. I was an experienced performer but I had always been one of five girls. Going solo meant being the centre of attention which appealed to me but was very scary. It was great to have George with me when the nerves started to kick in backstage — he'd seen it all before and reassured me I could do it.

Disaster was quite possible given my amazing lack of preparation. I had very little time to rehearse and not much material. I was working with the choreographer Luca Tommassini who I had collaborated with on the 'Look At Me' video, so we had the routine for that song but had to come up with the rest of the choreography when we met up the night before. By the time we were ready to go on stage, the audience was in a real frenzy. I was nervous about the performance but there was a lot of love coming up from the crowd so I decided I would just try and enjoy myself. 'Look At Me' started up and the place exploded. As I emerged onto the stage, the crowd were calling my name and the adrenalin rush kicked in. It had been a long time since I'd been on stage but it was all coming back to me, even if it was real seat-of-the-pants stuff. The highlight was my performance of 'My Heart Belongs To Daddy'. I pulled guys up on stage, asked their name and then straddled each of them, singing the song and pledging my heart directly to them. It was a real buzz and as I had hoped, the audience at G.A.Y made it a great atmosphere.

It was a relief that something had gone right because there was more disappointment to come. As with the single, I had hoped that my album would be Number One. The Spice Girls had done it and I wanted *Schizophonic* to repeat the feat so I was pretty gutted when it only made it to Number Four. It wasn't as big a blow as it had been with the single but it was disappointing because I had very high hopes.

I had always known that releasing an album would lay myself open to further criticism so I had a mixture of feelings when the record came out. I was really nervous because I had so much to prove and the songs were so personal. The album reflected all the different emotions and moods I'd experienced in the months since I left the group. On the sleeve I divided the songs into two sides — one red, one white. Red is for hot and for ego, and white is more spiritual and emotional. 'Look At Me' was on the red side but the songs that meant most to me were on the white side, like 'Someone's Watching Over Me', which was about my dad and my belief that he's up there looking down on me.

Dad's death was still extremely raw for me and I wasn't any closer to dealing with it. I received no counselling or help when he died and it was a rude awakening to lose him so suddenly. Even though he was 72, his heart attack came out of the blue and was a terrible shock. I was ill-equipped to deal with the loss or the sense of my own mortality that I felt. The song talks about how I often imagined Dad watching me and how, every time I did something in my career, I'd say, 'This is for you, Dad.' Somehow that helped.

Dad had always encouraged me to sing and dance and I thought that I could win his love by being a shining star. Dad had always done the best he could but I found it hard to feel his love and always wanted more. I remember finding it difficult when he would disappear into his workshop or behind his newspaper for hours and not be available. I needed constant confirmation that I was loved. I was born that way. Now I was still trying to make him proud even though he was gone.

I always want my songs to be real, so I draw on my life. I really poured my heart into 'Walk Away', which was about my mixed emotions over leaving the Spice Girls. I wanted to express the combination of fear and self-belief I felt as I stepped out on my own. I was saying 'I'm really scared but I think I can make it on my own'. There's one line that talks about 'walking away from emptiness'. I wasn't saying that the Spice Girls experience was empty because it wasn't, but it was an acknowledgement that I felt pretty empty by the end, no matter how much success we had achieved.

It was also a song about expressing emotions that had been bottled up. The only time I had been able to cry since leaving was when I was watching a video of *Dead Man Walking*, the drama about a convict on death row, starring Susan Sarandon and Sean Penn. I cried my eyes out. But I wasn't really crying over the movie, I was crying about the girls. 'Walk Away' was my attempt to reflect those feelings.

When I sat down and heard the completed album, I felt a real sense of achievement. The whole thing had come together very quickly because I was so eager to get it done. I knew it wasn't perfect but I was proud of it. Not bad for a first attempt, I thought.

As I stood in the sweltering heat of the Manila slums that June, surrounded by bewildered-looking market-stall owners fighting off an over-eager press pack, I realised that being a United Nations goodwill ambassador was a real job. I was in one of the most devout Catholic countries in the world, about to make a speech about contraception and safe sex that would kick off an almighty row. I may have been an ambassador but I wasn't too sure about the goodwill part on that particular day.

The UN had called me earlier on that year to ask me to go to the Philippines to support one of their sister organisations, Marie Stopes International, who provide reproductive health care in the developing world. Being given a job to do made the whole thing feel real. Up until then, my impressive UN ambassador title had been something to make my mum proud but hadn't involved me actually *doing* anything. Now I had to go out there and do it.

The Philippines is a devoutly Catholic country and the Church is very powerful and influential. It was a controversial place to go to talk about contraception, safe sex and reproductive rights but it has one of the fastest-growing populations in the world so the need was urgent. I knew it was a Catholic country and that my message might be controversial but I'd said I wanted to get my hands dirty and this was my chance. When they heard I was going on this trip the producers of *Geri's World Walkabout* saw an opportunity to do some more filming for the show during my two-day stay.

I wasn't in the best of shape for the trip. To be honest, I was knackered. I was still in the middle of promotional work which hadn't really stopped since the eight-day tour around the world two months before. I was also dealing with the disappointment of the chart positions and the stress of the documentary broadcast which was scheduled for a second showing the following week. I wasn't really prepared for what I was about to run into.

As soon as I arrived in Manila, I was knocked sideways by the oppressively sticky heat and the madness and bustle of the city itself. I had experienced the hassle of busy cities and hot weather before — it came with the pop-star territory — but this was culture shock. I arrived at the hotel feeling stressed out and nervous about what lay ahead.

The first part of my trip was a visit to a family planning clinic in Manila which was hidden away in a back-street slum in the middle of a fruit and vegetable market. I had seen poverty in Africa when I was in Uganda for Comic Relief, but there was something about the filth of urban poverty that was even more upsetting. As luck would have it, today was market day. I picked my way through the stalls with my UN minder, sweat pouring down my back and overpowered by the smell. I felt so guilty because following immediately behind us were what seemed like hundreds of film crews and reporters. It was a media scrum and they were trampling over the market stalls, knocking over the cabbages and the noodle stands, calling to get my attention and get a shot of me. It was chaos. The local people were trying to earn what living they could and my trip was disrupting everything.

The clinic was a place where women could go to get check-ups and advice. It was there for mothers and young girls seeking contraceptive advice as well as for prostitutes or massage-parlour workers needing AIDS tests or free condoms. I met a woman who was still in her twenties and had five children. She was younger than me but she had come in to discuss sterilisation. It was a different world.

I came out of the clinic to find that there were even more people waiting outside for me. The locals had seen the film crews and came over to see what was going on so the place was overrun. Perfect conditions for me to make my statement! A microphone was set up for me in front of the clinic and there were people climbing up on roofs, looking down on me from all vantage points. The heat was intense as I squeezed my way out in front of the crowd and tried to compose myself.

'I believe that everybody deserves the right to have control of their life,' I started, my voice struggling to be heard above the hubbub, 'and that means having control over your fertility. That means being able to have protection against disease and unwanted pregnancy. That is everybody's fundamental right.'

These were pretty controversial words for a country where 84 percent of the population are Catholic, but the crowd hardly raised a murmur. What was going on? Maybe I'd won them all over with the power of my argument and they were having to rethink the way they looked at the issue? Unfortunately that wasn't the reason. The crowd was just staring at me blankly because they didn't speak English and nobody had the faintest idea what I was talking about! They must have been wondering who this woman was rambling on in English and disrupting their Monday morning market. The only people who did hear what I was saying were the media and they were quick to spread the word.

Later on that day, I met a group of sixteen-year-olds at a local college who were a real-life example of girl power. They had written to the government saying they wanted some education in sexual health. They were getting support from Marie Stopes but needed someone to speak up for them and I was happy to do so. When I arrived, there were all these Filipino kids cheering me and we sat down and really talked about the issues. I was very inexperienced as an ambassador but I did realise how delicate the situation was in the Philippines. I had a Catholic upbringing and I knew that it was dangerous to be saying that I believed people should be educated about safe sex and contraception. I just thought it had to be said and so did these Filipino girls.

The reaction started to come through after my statement outside the clinic was reported on TV and in the newspapers. The head of the Catholic Church in the Philippines, Cardinal Sin — I'm not making this up, that really was his name — was very upset. He is passionately opposed to contraception and abortion and once said that condoms were 'evil', so I was never going to be *his* favourite Spice Girl. The Cardinal had really done his homework because he told the papers: 'We understand her album as well as her singing career is in jeopardy.' I was flattered he paid such close attention! Not to be outdone, the Mayor of Manila joined in. 'What right does she have to come here and talk to people about what to do with their bodies and families?' he asked. 'Is she supposed to be a model of British morals for us to copy? This former porno pin-up model is telling our people, our children and minors what is right and wrong in how they have their families.' Charming!

As the media storm hit, I did feel under threat because of the strength of feeling about the issue. I started to worry that there might be some fundamentalist elements who hated me for what I was doing and would want to put a bomb under my car, shoot me or stab me or something. Even though I was driven around in a diplomat's car, I didn't have a guard. It was frightening because whenever I appeared in public people screamed and banged on the car roof and windows. This wasn't unusual for me — it had happened since my time in the Spice Girls — but as the controversy grew I did begin to realise that these weren't the usual high spirits of overenthusiastic fans but something more sinister.

I can understand why some people felt angry but I think my views were misunderstood and mis-represented. I didn't want to tell people what to think. I have no problem with people being against contraception or abortion. They have a right to their point of view and I respect that those are the views of the Catholic Church. I am sure there are Catholic girls who aren't having sex before marriage and will only have unprotected sex in a monogamous relationship. I respect that, but the bottom line is that there are unmarried Catholic girls who get pregnant and contract AIDS because they have sex without condoms. I think that speaks for itself.

My view is that people should have the right to be educated about these things and, if they decide that using contraception is the right thing for them, they should be allowed to do so. People should be given the choice and it's usually women who suffer if those choices aren't available.

I didn't think it was possible to see poverty more shocking than the slums I had seen on my first day but I was wrong. I did some filming for *Geri's World Walkabout* at a massive rubbish dump on the outskirts of town. The rubbish rose up in huge steaming mountains over an area of two miles and the mounds of trash were covered with people — mostly kids — scavenging for anything of value. That was bad enough but then I realised that people actually *lived* there as well. This rubbish tip was their home, their work, their life.

I have never experienced a smell like it. Just being there made me want to be physically sick because it was so overwhelming. I met a sixteen-year-old girl called Jessica who had lived on the rubbish tip all her life. She had lived through hell. She told me that once, when she was eight years old, she had found a bag full of dead foetuses. It was such a horrific story and it seemed to bring the whole issue full circle. This was the reality and it just broke my heart. It said everything to me about the importance of the issues I was there to campaign about.

It was so difficult to do justice to Jessica's story. I felt inadequate because I didn't really know how to emotionally respond to such things. How could I? I felt so much sympathy and respect for her but my life and the opportunities I had were so far removed from hers. How could I justify that? All I could do was my little bit — and I told myself that was better than doing nothing — but I still felt an overwhelming sense of hopelessness.

When I left the country I felt very upset about the whole experience. My trip had stirred up a lot of emotion and anger in other people and I hadn't set out to upset anyone. When I got home I went to my mum's house in Watford to talk it all through. Mum — who is a Catholic — sat me down at the kitchen table and made me a cup of tea. 'You know what, Geri?' she said. 'If you cause a little bit of uproar in the Philippines and upset the Catholic Church, it doesn't matter because if what you've done helps just one girl avoid unwanted pregnancy or disease then it's worth it. Just one girl makes it worthwhile.'

I could have done with a rest after the stress and controversy of the Philippines but the promotional bandwagon rolled on. There was now pressure to choose a new single and it had to be the right one. The situation wasn't made any easier by the fact that it hadn't worked out with my manager Lisa Anderson.

My timing's always very bad and I'm not always practical in my thinking but I realised things weren't working out with Lisa so I decided I had to make a change. Lisa is a wonderful person and we are still friends but I felt she had too much on her plate to look after me, what with running the Brits, living down in Kent and bringing up a family. It wasn't the best time to make a change — in the middle of promo! But, just like when I left the Spice Girls, once my mind was made up that was it.

I didn't have time to think about who else I could bring in at such short notice, so I decided that I would try and cope with managing myself, at least until I had time to work out a more permanent arrangement. I had my little computer and my PA Victoria (who had left the Spice Girls to work for me) and things seemed to just about hold together but it was a new layer of stress to add to everything else. Every day when I'd come home from being pop star Geri Halliwell, I'd have to sit in the office and go through the paperwork. I was getting requests right, left and centre and it was exhausting keeping on top of it all.

This was a make or break moment for my career. The disappointing way in which the single and album had sold had become the story. Some press reports were positively gleeful about the prospect that Geri's fifteen minutes of fame were up. It felt like I had one more shot at solo success or else I would be facing retirement from the world of pop at the grand old age of 26.

I had always gone with my instinct when it came to choosing singles. It hadn't worked last time round but I decided to follow my heart again. The record company wanted me to go with 'Lift Me Up' and the Absolute boys thought 'Bag It Up' but I was convinced that 'Mi Chico Latino' was the one. I played it to a few people to get their point of view and I remember getting the thumbs up from Lisa Anderson's little girl when I did the kid test on her.

I had written the song with the Absolute boys in the autumn of 1998. I'd always listened to a lot of Latin music because of my mum and I wanted to do something with a Spanish influence for her. That day in the studio, we had a melody but we didn't have any words. So I called my mum from the studio to see if she could help.

'Mum,' I said, 'what do you say to a bloke in Spanish if you fancy him and are being romantic?'

There was a sigh at the end of the line and she said, 'Oh Geri, I can't remember that far back, it's so long ago.'

So I asked her to have a look at her extensive library of Spanish language slushy romances and she just read the titles out to me. Eventually she came out with '*¿Dónde está el hombre con fuego en la sangre?*'

'Oh, what does that mean, Mum?' I asked, liking the way it sounded.

'Where is the man with the fire in his blood?' she said, and that was the start of the song. So I had my mum and her romantic paperbacks to thank for that and I took it from there. Mum loves the song, so it is very special to me.

I wanted the video for 'Chico' to be very different in style to 'Look At Me' and not just for creative reasons. 'Look At Me' was filmed in Prague in the freezing cold and was a very long and complicated shoot. I was determined that this time I was going to do the video somewhere warm. I also wanted it to be a simple and straightforward video because I realised that no one really understood or even noticed the ideas I'd put into 'Look At Me'. In a video it's blink and you miss it so why make it hard on myself? Instead I thought I'd cut to the chase and shoot the video off the coast of Sardinia on a yacht with some very cute male dancers!

The location was stunning. The yacht, weather and sea were all beautiful. It was wonderful sitting around on the boat with just a few others aboard and we had some really lovely times relaxing in the sunshine and chatting on the warm nights. The dancers came on the yacht for the filming and then left, leaving the rest of us to have a meal before going to our cabins for the night. On the first day of filming, we were doing sequences on the beach and there were people raking the sand. I thought they were being a bit over-meticulous about making the beach look perfect. They didn't tell me until afterwards that the real reason was that there were jellyfish everywhere. In retrospect, it was probably best that I didn't know!

Being on a boat with a team of scantily clad dancers demanded that I wore a bikini for the video. I had become as tired of demure and dull Geri as I had been of slapstick sexy Ginger and I felt ready to be just a little bit more naturally sexy and sensual. I was still very curvy but less bloated and more toned than I had been in the Spice Girls and I wanted to be sexy without being slutty. That was all very well in theory but it went to the heart of my problems with body image and diet. The thought of being on screen wearing so little and under such scrutiny was terrifying. As a solo artist I would be in 90 percent of the shots and I felt I had to look terrific to carry that off.

I have always dieted to prepare for an occasion but this time I really started cutting back on my food in a big way. I would pretend it was a 'detox' but that was such a load of crap. It was pretty much starvation. I'd live on fruit like melon for days and obsessively work out just thinking about how I had to get slim in time for the video shoot. It wasn't as if I was cutting back from a normal diet either. I had been using SlimFast to take the place of a normal lunch on and off for a year and I was following the Dr Atkins diet by then. But not content with limiting the carbohydrates, I was cutting back on fat as well. I was trying to keep my food completely squeaky-clean.

I could manage this sort of regime on and off and when I did I would lose a lot of weight in about two weeks. I also got bad breath and constipation. It drained my energy but I was so unaware of my body that I just thought I was tired because my lifestyle gave me so many reasons to feel that way. The furthest thing from my mind was that it had anything to do with eating or, more to the point, not eating. Then I would weaken and come off it and put the weight back on again. When I came off the wagon I would overeat on all the food I was craving, to compensate for the long periods when I denied myself. So regardless of how I was looking, I was not in the best of health because of the diet I was already on and cutting back even more to look good in a bikini was very dangerous.

Once we got underway with the filming for the video I started to relax. My mind was telling me that I had succeeded by getting as far as the shoot and that I had earned the right to indulge a little. I had worked hard to get slim enough for a bikini and I found being in front of the camera wearing one very stressful. The prospect of food was like my reward for effort and relief from stress.

One beautiful Mediterranean evening we were on the yacht enjoying a meal when I started to eat the bread from the basket in the middle of the table. Bread was against my rules but that was part of the reason I wanted to eat it so much. It felt naughty allowing myself to indulge in such a forbidden pleasure and gradually I filled myself up on the illicit carbohydrate. After I'd eaten a few slices, I started to feel a bit bloated and I started to worry about it showing up on the shoot in the morning. It would ruin the video if I looked fatter on one part than the other. The others were deep in conversation, so I excused myself from the table quietly and went below deck to the boat's toilet. When I got there, I got down on my knees, stuck my fingers down my throat and was violently sick.

Since leaving the Spice Girls I had overeaten on a few occasions but had not made myself sick. I had raided the mini-bar in the Philippines because that was my response when things got a little too much to handle. Most people go and have a drink to unwind and relax but I'd go and put some food in my mouth to sedate myself and take the edge off.

For months my regular diet had been salmon and vegetables. Most days I would eat that and little or nothing else. Sometimes I would even have salmon for breakfast if I wasn't skipping the meal altogether. I'd never have any potatoes. It would be the same food over and over again and it was so boring. When I restricted my diet like that, I was inevitably on my way to a binge which is exactly what had happened on the boat that night.

So the video got made and I got a huge amount of attention from it. People came up to me and told me how great I looked and how sexy it was. They also told me I looked really healthy, but how wrong they were. I wasn't healthy because I wasn't eating properly and although I was slim at the time, that was a mirage too because the tough regime of the diet was always going to lead me to binge and put the weight back on.

On the plane home from Sardinia I tried to come to terms with what had happened. I had really believed I had my bulimia licked. I'd even talked to others about how I'd beaten it, to help them get over it as I had done. So, I told myself that this episode was a one-off and that I wouldn't succumb again. In reality, I was kidding myself, the facts were obvious — my bulimia was back.

Number One

It was hard to tell what the crowd were thinking. I was halfway through my first song, 'Look At Me', and I could feel the rain that had threatened all day finally starting to fall. It wasn't too much of a problem for me because I was holding a little pink umbrella to go with my bare feet, fake tan and curly blonde hair extensions. I was more worried about the 100,000 people standing in the rain in the middle of Hyde Park. The thing is, it's difficult to judge the mood of such an enormous crowd from high up on the stage, so I had no idea how I was going down. Is that someone dancing down there or are they just trying to keep warm in the rain?

I had only arrived back from the video shoot in Sardinia with hours to spare before my appearance at the biggest gig of my life. Even when I was with the Spice Girls, I had never played to an audience this large and my only previous solo performance had been at G.A.Y earlier in the summer. It was packed that night but the Astoria has a capacity of just a few thousand. Party in the Park 1999 was in a different league.

I was sharing an impressive bill with Shania Twain, Ricky Martin and Boyzone but, for the press at least, I was the focus of a lot of the attention because at just about the time I would be taking to the stage, Victoria was to become Mrs David Beckham. The press was full of speculation about whether I had been invited to the wedding or whether I had chosen to stay away. I didn't want to give the 'debate' about it oxygen so I chose not to comment. I've never seen two people more devoted to each other than David and Victoria and, no matter what the press wanted to make out, I was really happy for them.

It was always very difficult for me whenever there were any reports about the girls in the press because I missed them and would have liked it to be easier for us to enjoy a closer relationship. The media were always keen to play up rifts or disagreements between us but I just tried my best to stay out of it. There were often reports in the paper about comments that one or other of the girls was supposed to have made that were critical of me or my music. When I read things like that I thought of the many occasions when I had said something to a journalist that had got twisted and taken out of context and I just assumed that the same thing had happened to them. I wanted to give the girls the benefit of the doubt because things can be said as a joke which look serious on paper. I would try to ignore it for self-preservation's sake.

In the end, it's between us. The girls and I are not as close as we were but we have spoken occasionally since I left the group. We are like university graduates who go their separate ways and watch with interest how the others are doing. Whatever relationships I have with them are not with the Spice Girls: they are with Melanie, Melanie, Victoria and Emma.

Whatever else was going on that Sunday in July, I had my own big day to get through. My preparation left something to be desired to say the least because the schedule had not permitted any rehearsal time. I had to rely on the routines we had used for the G.A.Y show. I had three songs to do: 'Chico', 'Look At Me' and 'Bag It Up', and I was running late to meet up with the dancers and Luca, my choreographer, in a hotel opposite Hyde Park. As I arrived Luca was in a bit of a panic.

'Come on, Geri,' he said, 'we have to be on stage in ten minutes!' So I rushed upstairs to the hotel suite we had booked to give us somewhere to practise. I needed particular help from Luca on 'Bag It Up' because I just couldn't remember how it went. 'Have you got it?' Luca asked as we finished the run-through.

'Um, not sure, really,' I said, 'but it'll have to do. We were supposed to be on stage two minutes ago.'

So that was the end of the rehearsal and we had to run as fast as we could across Hyde Park to get to the stage. We were the next act on.

The scary thing about Party in the Park is that you are not singing to your own fans alone. Only some of them have come to see you, so I was worried that they'd hate me or that some of them hated me already. I had decided to go barefoot — which the papers called the 'glamorous gypsy look' — because I'd just seen the movie *Barefoot in the Park* and I thought it would make a cute headline.

I had very little time in the dressing room and was ushered up to the side of the stage almost as soon as I arrived backstage. That was when the fear and anticipation really hit me — all those people waiting to see if I had what it takes. It's like going to a party when you are a teenager and feeling a combination of fear and excitement. I wanted to be the belle of the ball but I had to overcome my fear to pull it off. I found the best way was to imagine the worst-case scenario — falling over — and be willing to accept that fate should it await me. Once I had done that it was possible get through the fear.

Luckily, as soon as I skipped onto the stage looking like a little pixie with my bare feet and my pink umbrella, my experience started to kick in. The adrenalin buzz of being on stage is the greatest there is and I felt it pretty much immediately. Once you get through the fear it is like breaking through to the other side — it hurts but once you are there it is brilliant. As my first song came to an end, I was about to find out what the crowd thought of me. The relief was fantastic when the crowd roared its approval. It seemed they weren't going to be downhearted by a bit of rain and they didn't blame me for it! It was such a confidence boost to receive the crowd's appreciation and know that whatever I read in the papers and whatever doubts I had, people *did* still like what I do. Getting my breath back, I looked out into the park and asked. 'Have you missed me?'

The crowd's screams seemed to be saying, 'Yes!'

'You really know how to make a girl feel wanted,' I replied, feeling like I was flirting with 100,000 people, and as we started 'Mi Chico Latino' — my make or break new single — I started to enjoy myself.

I am a crowd-pleaser and I have the gift of being able to win a crowd round and keep them having fun. I think the key is not to wobble and to always give the impression that you are comfortable and having a great time and, if you're not, fake it. Sometimes the crowd needs a kick up the arse from the performer, or permission to party, and I know how to do that. I gave the crowd a little bit of a push that day because I wanted them to like me and have a good time — I will always try every trick in the book to make that happen.

It was an important day for me because I realised that this was what my job was about — having fun and giving other people some light relief. I felt cheeky and light-hearted again — doing my pixie act with a smile and a twinkle and a sense of humour and then leaving. I think people had forgotten what I do and, after the documentary and the sensible shoes, who could blame them? That day at Party in the Park I reminded them that Geri Halliwell was a pop star and a pretty good one when she puts her mind to it!

I woke up the next day feeling completely invigorated. I had decided a couple of months before that I would throw myself a big party for my 27th birthday and had planned it for the day before 'Mi Chico Latino' was released. I grew up in a family that had very little money and because for a long period of time my mother was a Jehovah's Witness, and they don't celebrate birthdays, I have no real memory of having birthday parties or celebrations as a child. I definitely had a birthday dinner with my family on my seventeenth birthday because I can remember getting my provisional driving licence but apart from that they simply hadn't featured.

So I decided to make up for lost time and to hold a party at home at St Paul's. The house and grounds were so huge it seemed a waste to have me rattling around in there alone and this was an ideal opportunity to inject some life into the place. I decided that it would be fantastic to have my own fairground. It was just the kind of thing you want when you are a kid and finally I had my chance. I had been working on the party for a couple of months and had arranged for a massive marquee and a big wheel, bumper cars and a bucking bronco. We even installed a Sumo wrestling ring where you put on a fat suit and grapple with your partner until one of you chucks the other out.

I had invited 300 people but as the big day approached, I started to get really worried that no one would turn up and it would all be a massive embarrassment. Even when there is no reason to worry there is always a little pang of insecurity and fear but on the day of the party I actually became convinced the whole thing would be a flop. The party was due to start at one o'clock and go on into the night, so I got up early to put the finishing touches to everything. I looked out of the window that morning and it was absolutely chucking it down with rain. I was mortified, convinced that only a handful of people would come because of the terrible English summer weather, and there I'd be, riding the bumper cars on my own.

Then at one o'clock on the dot, the rain stopped and the sun came out. I was so relieved and, gradually, people started to arrive. There were friends and family and lots of children. Dawn French and Lenny Henry came with their kids and Matthew Freud and his family were there along with celebrities like Lulu and Jamie Theakston. George was there and he brought me the most amazing birthday present I have ever been given. It was a 1960s navy-blue Mercedes convertible which he drove onto the lawn to present to me. It was fantastic! He had a similar car that I loved to drive around when I visited him in the South of France and he knew how much I would love one of my own. I christened it my Grace Kelly car.

Everyone had a great time. The field was wet, my trousers got soaked and I said goodbye to any hopes of a beautiful lawn with perfect straight lines but it was worth it. They say you never enjoy your own parties but I didn't do too badly. I remember having a laugh with Jamie Theakston on a ride called the Monster and playing an adult pass-the-parcel game with forfeits like having to do ten press-ups on top of the person next to you or changing clothes with your neighbour. Then, at the end of the evening, we had a disco and got drunk. It was great. It was the party to make up for all the lost birthday parties.

In the evening my birthday cake was brought out. It had 27 candles and I made a wish when I blew them out. Everyone knew that I wanted 'Mi Chico Latino' to go to the top of the charts because so much was riding on it, so I said, 'I think you know what I want for my birthday,' then closed my eyes, blew out the candles and wished. I think the whole party held onto that wish for me.

No matter what the experts and pundits said about my prospects, I was feeling fairly confident about the chances of 'Chico' doing well. First and foremost I thought it was a good record. It was poppy and catchy and perfect for the summer. I think my core audience is young teenage girls and gay guys. Both of those groups tend to like pure pop music and I think that's what 'Chico' was. It was very different from the slightly leftfield style of 'Look At Me' and the video was also pretty easy to get — a yacht, a girl in a bikini and some sexy boy dancers to keep both sets of fans happy.

The other thing that 'Chico' had going for it was that the music was Latin-based. I had written the song back in 1998 but by the time the summer of 1999 came around Latin-influenced music was ruling the charts. Ricky Martin had recently had a Number One and there were others on the way. So it was a strange example of synchronicity that I should be ready to go with a Latin track which I had written almost a year before. I sometimes think that there is something in the air that can influence you months before you realise it and I think that's what happened with 'Chico'. The time was right.

So I was confident but not 100 percent certain that I would make it. The waiting is the worst part so I decided to go down to George and Kenny's villa in St Tropez and sit it out in the sunshine. It's a lovely place and I always found it relaxing to hang out there and wander around in the beautiful gardens, especially when there was something on my mind. When you release a record on a Monday you get the first sales figures through on Tuesday or Wednesday and from those they work out a 'midweek' chart position. I was in George's little white kitchen and had just gone to the well-stocked fridge to get my second SlimFast of the day — one for breakfast, one for lunch — when I got a call from EMI saying, 'You're 20,000 ahead, you're the midweek Number One.' It was such a great feeling but you never know what might happen. Experience told me I was unlikely to be overtaken because the gap was so big but I was still a nervous wreck about it. With the nerves and the SlimFast I was losing a lot of weight.

I spent the rest of the week just hanging out with Kenny or my sister Natalie who had come down to see me. It was the perfect place to kill time but the paparazzi are never far away. One day, Natalie and I were sunbathing by George's pool when, out of the corner of my eye, I saw some movement coming from a nearby bush. I got up and walked towards it thinking there might be an animal in there. Then suddenly I saw a paparazzo pointing his camera at me. I literally jumped in shock and screamed at him. It seemed to work because he started running. I don't know what I planned to do if I caught him but I gave chase in my little bikini, haring across George's beautifully manicured lawn, trying to get hold of him. Given how angry I was, that man was lucky to get away.

Then, on the Sunday, the call came through from the EMI office. I had made it! 'Chico' was number one. With that and Party in the Park, it looked like my career was back on track. I didn't really allow myself to relish the success or to stick my fingers up at anyone who had doubted me because I was just so relieved. Once something is over, good or bad, I am always on to the next thing. I wasn't able to just settle down and enjoy the present moment as much as I maybe should have. Now I had got to the top I had a new problem — how could I repeat the feat next time round? Almost straight away I started thinking about what the next single should be.

I had responded to the return of my bulimia on the video shoot by trying to be even more obsessive and controlling about the food I ate. During the day I was surviving on SlimFast and fruit. In the evenings I would usually eat a normal meal with George and Kenny but my eating habits were totally driven by the desire to lose more weight. I was completely obsessive. My mind was telling me that 'When I'm thin my life will begin' and I was very sensitive about my weight and body image.

Soon after the record went to Number One, I remember standing in George's living room watching TV having yet another SlimFast. There's a programme called MTVSelect which is hosted by pop bands and this one afternoon they had the boy band Another Level presenting. My video for 'Chico' came on and I was watching myself on the yacht with the dancers and enjoying the success for a moment, thinking I looked pretty good. When the song finished it cut back to Another Level in the studio discussing the video. One of the guys — I don't know his name — said, 'Yeah, she looks kinda fit now, don't she? Now she's lost a bit of weight.' It was just so cutting and it confirmed my feeling that I had been fat before and that the dieting was necessary. I remember standing there watching it with the can of SlimFast in my hand feeling absolutely hideous. He was saying that I was a little bit more acceptable now that I'd lost a few pounds, which was exactly how I felt about myself.

A few months later I was on promo doing a big show in Germany and Another Level were one of the other acts on. I was at the TV studio when I saw them coming along the corridor. We didn't really know each other but they said 'Hi ya!' because that's what you do when you have a corridor moment like that, so I put on a really insincere and over-nice voice and said, 'Hi-iiii and thanks a lot.' They had no idea what I meant so one of them said, 'OK but what for?'

'For calling me fat on MTV.'

Their mouths dropped open and they started back-pedalling as fast as they could. They were saying they didn't mean it that way and that they were very sorry, so I let them sweat for a while and then said 'It's alright, don't worry about it' and walked away. But the truth was, it had really hurt.

Controlling food was just one thing I was obsessive about at that time. For a while I was compulsively shopping too. This wasn't your average retail therapy but involved me obsessively buying expensive underwear. It sounds ridiculous but I could not stop buying the stuff. At one point I was spending £200 a day on underwear. I would feel that I had to buy different colours of knickers and bras: sexy ones, regular ones, big ones, small ones. I would get people to bring them to me or I would go out and buy them. Whenever I felt dissatisfaction or was upset, I'd go shopping. At the time, though, I just thought it was funny. There was never a moment where I looked at the credit card bill or at the piles and piles of bras and knickers and thought that this was strange or unusual behaviour. It was like a fix.

I knew things weren't right because of how I felt inside but I couldn't understand how this related to spending hundreds of pounds in underwear shops. It was the same old story. Inside I was feeling empty and I suppose I thought it would fill me up. In fact, any lift I got from retail therapy quickly faded and the more I bought the less the buzz.

I had no sense of balance when it came to money. I would swing from feeling fearful because I might overspend to extreme recklessness. I went to an auction for the Prince's Trust around this time and found myself sitting down with all these really well-off people. I remember sticking my hand up and getting into a bidding war for the rent of a Jaguar for a year. I didn't need the car but that didn't matter, it wasn't the point. I just did it for its own sake and I ended up spending £10,000 on something I didn't want and didn't need. It was madness.

To an extent my friends and family were sheltered from the worst excesses of my obsessive behaviour because I tried to keep them private. But Kenny and my interior designer friend Linda *were* concerned about me. One day I was with Linda discussing some ideas for St Paul's when she brought the conversation round to relationships.

'The thing is, Geri,' she said, 'you mustn't isolate yourself. I think it's about time you started getting active and getting out there. You are being far too insular.' Linda had seen how driven I had been by my career since leaving the group and now, with the success of the single, she saw it as a chance for me to look at the other priorities in life. Kenny was more straightforward.

'Geri, I think it's time you went out there and found a man.'

Like most of us, when I think about the future I imagine starting a family. I would love to get married and have children one day. Before I get there, though, there's the small matter of finding the right guy.

I hadn't had a really serious relationship since I was 21 when I broke up with a guy from Watford called Sean who I had been going out with for two and a half years. Since then, I'd had little flings and affairs but nothing serious. I don't think I'd ever really fallen in love although I had been infatuated with people on more than a few occasions. The early days are always a wonderful time in a relationship because you are caught up in the whirlwind and spend your time thinking about the other person as much as yourself, which is very good for the soul. After that stage, though, my relationships hadn't ever really developed. A point comes after a month or two where it's either going to take off or it isn't and mine just never had.

Despite my own experiences, I believe in marriage and I am a romantic. But I feel sorry for women because I think men are fundamentally not monogamous. I think that those primal differences between men wanting to spread their seed as far and wide as possible and women wanting to find their one mate will always be in conflict. That doesn't mean I think all relationships are doomed to failure. Deep down I believe that love can conquer all and if you fall in love, you can find a way to make it work.

I was used to not being in a relationship. In fact, it felt easier not to be in one, but when Linda and Kenny suggested I get out there and date, I was open to the idea. It felt like a good time because my career could take a back seat for a little while and because I knew I needed more than just material success to be truly happy. I think lots of people want another person to come along and fix them and many women think, If only I had a boyfriend I'd be happy, and I was as likely to believe that as anyone.

At the same time my recent success had given me a confidence boost. I was feeling more alive and open than I had in a long time. I finally felt able to get out there and parade myself, like a peacock showing its feathers. So I made a decision to look for boys to date and to accept the chance when friends offered to fix me up with someone. I am quite shy in those situations and I can be nervous in the company of someone new but I gave it a go anyway. They were all blind dates arranged by friends and friends of friends and although I had some pleasant enough evenings, nothing really worked out. I just didn't click with anyone I met.

Then, out of the blue, someone came along and pursued me.

I had always found Chris Evans attractive. He was a bit of a pin-up for me because he was such an inspirational person and sometimes those qualities outweigh more superficial attractions like looks or sophistication.

When I was a wannabe, I used to have a notice board in the kitchen of my little studio flat in Watford dedicated to those people whose footsteps I wanted to follow in. Alongside Marlene Dietrich and Marilyn Monroe, I had a picture of Planet 24 TV producer Charlie Parsons and one of his star presenters, Chris Evans. Those two represented a spirit of originality and making it against the odds that inspired me. These were the people who had really seized the day and broken new ground and I loved them for it.

Chris was actually behind my debut on national television when he chose to air a hugely embarrassing audition tape I had sent into *The Big Breakfast* in the early nineties. In the video I was trying out for a job as a presenter on a new entertainment show and was interviewing two American footballers in London. I conducted the interview in the pouring rain with mascara running down my face and made a terrible mess of the whole thing. The fact that the two Americans were pulling faces at me behind my back and trying to grab my arse hadn't helped either. When they showed it on *The Big Breakfast* as a joke, Chris seemed to find it very funny.

Things weren't much better when it came to the Spice Girls. I remember how hurt I was in the early days when Mel B and I went to meet Suzie Aplin, a producer from Chris's *TFI Friday* programme, to see if we could get on the show. While we were talking to Suzie, Chris appeared at the window. We looked up at him expectantly but all he did was mouth the words, 'Why don't you just go back to *Live & Kicking*?' At the time Chris had the power to break bands on his TV and radio shows and the fact that he thought the Spice Girls were just for kids was a real knock back.

To his credit, Chris changed his mind a few years later when he saw us perform at Wembley and publicly apologised for getting it so wrong. The few times we'd met in those days we always enjoyed each other's company. He was also very supportive when I left the group and helped me work out what I was going to do by discussing my TV options with me. Although I had always admired him and valued his opinion, there had been nothing romantic between us.

That autumn of 1999, I was being interviewed on Radio One about my career and about music in general when the DJ asked me how I defined a good record. I answered that my rule of thumb was that if a song still sounds good ten years after it came out then you know it's a great record. As it turned out, Chris had been listening to the interview and he called me to say how much he agreed with the comment and asked me if I fancied meeting up. Later we went out. I thought he was charming, interesting and funny and after that we started seeing a lot of each other and hanging out all the time. We were just doing the usual things that normal people do when they start dating — going to restaurants and walking in the park. The only difference for us was that, at the same time, we were hiding from the press, trying to keep our relationship a secret.

During the first few weeks we were spotted together and there was a bit of speculation and rumour flying around but luckily nothing reached the newspapers. We knew it had to come out sooner or later but it was great to have this little secret from the world even though it was inevitable that it would only be for a short period of time. I was about to step back onto the promotional treadmill for my third single, 'Lift Me Up', which was scheduled for a November release. That meant doing lots of media at the end of October and this activity was going to make it very difficult to keep things quiet and avoid the paparazzi getting pictures of us together. Sure enough, on 21st October, Chris and I were snapped driving off in Chris's Ferrari and the speculation started in earnest. The following day, I was booked onto one of the most high-profile TV shows in Britain — *TFI Friday*. It was my appearance on the show that night that really set tongues wagging.

It was a strange experience because I was going to be interviewed by Chris on the show about my album and book *If Only* but at the same time we had this thing going on that nobody really knew about. There was speculation but no one was sure if it was true or not. It was funny because it was like this little secret or in-joke that we had between us and there we were on national television acting as if we were just good friends. Having said that, the next day the press was full of stills of Chris kissing me as he welcomed me onto the show. The implication was that this was more than just a peck on the cheek and the press interest was really warming up.

As it turned out, my most passionate kiss of the evening was not with Chris at all. I have loved Kylie Minogue since watching her in *Neighbours*. I think she's cool and was happy she was going to be on *TFI* on the same night as me. There was this big phoney story going around that we were actually really competitive with each other because we were the two rival queens of pop fighting it out for the same market. In reality we got on really well. At the end of the show we were both sitting round the table and we decided to make a joke of it so, over the credits, we arm-wrestled to see which of the pop divas would triumph. After the arm-wrestle, when we were off-air, Kylie whispered to me, 'I know, why don't we kiss?' I thought it might be fun so I said 'OK' and we did. It was funny and the cameras had kept rolling so they showed it on the programme the following week. She's a great kisser and it distracted attention from me and Chris for a few more days.

The story really broke in early November when I was photographed leaving Chris's house in Belgravia. The paparazzi ended up getting countless pictures including private shots of us together, kissing in a restaurant, but the story of a relationship between two celebrities was not enough for the press. There had to be an angle and the release of my new single provided that.

After my first solo Number One I was hungry for another but it wasn't going to be easy because I had competition. By November 1999 Mel B and Mel C had both had successful solo singles. That meant that three out of the original five Spice Girls had had hits outside the group. The latest of the girls to try her hand at a solo career was Emma. The plan was for her to release a cover version of the old Edie Brickell hit *What I Am* with a group of dance producers called Tin Tin Out. The record was to be billed as Tin Tin Out 'featuring Emma B'. I was always pleased when one of the girls had a solo record out because it proved how talented the Spice Girls had been. The only problem was that Emma's single was scheduled for release on 7th November, the same day as mine. It was like Boyzone all over again and this time everyone was going to think it was personal.

Record release dates are set months in advance. The whole record company knows when singles are scheduled for release and 'Lift Me Up' was always set for a release date of 7th November and that never changed. Both of us were signed to EMI records — I was released through Chrysalis and Emma through Virgin — and I have no idea why but somehow the two singles had been scheduled to come out on the same day. Perhaps there was an accident or a mix-up because Emma's record was not released under her own name. I suppose that we were bound to run into each other at some point with four out of the original five girls out there doing their own thing, but it was an unfortunate clash. Now the stage was set for a high-profile battle between Ginger and Baby for the Number One spot. I was horrified.

Of course, the assumption was that it was all a big set-up engineered to drum up more publicity around the release of both singles. If it was, I wasn't aware of it. It just felt to me like an unnecessary complication. I didn't want it to become an acrimonious competition but the press were intent on hyping up some sort of competitive sibling cat fight. There was enough pressure releasing and promoting a single without that. Emma didn't need it — this was her first solo single, after all — and nor did I. The press played it for all it was worth, though, because it's a very easy story. It was like Blur v. Oasis all over again.

By the time I realised I was going up against Emma, it was too late to change the release date and I just had to turn my attention to getting the job done regardless. It was very hard to avoid getting caught up in the whole media circus around it and I would not be human if the whole fuss did not get to my ego. Although I didn't want to participate in the story of our rivalry, part of me was thinking, That's my ex-colleague, another Spice Girl, but I still want the Number One slot. It was natural I should feel like that but I felt a little guilty that I did.

The so-called 'battle' between Emma and I to get to Number One became the background to everything as far as the press were concerned. As soon as my relationship with Chris became public, the newspapers were determined to present it as an elaborate publicity stunt designed to get me to the top of the charts.

I can see why people would believe what the papers were saying about the relationship being a sham, a pantomime played out for the cameras and perfectly timed for maximum impact on our 'flagging' careers. I can understand why people thought it but they were wrong. The relationship was real. Chris and I were together and it had nothing to do with records or radio listeners or PR companies.

It wasn't really such a surprising situation. After all, relationships often start at work. If you are a girl working on the checkout at Tesco there's a good chance you might hook up with the guy who works behind the meat counter. Celebrities and entertainers are no different. The people I meet at work and who understand and can talk about the things I deal with in my working life tend to be famous people too. It was quite natural that Chris and I should get together.

It's always been difficult enough dealing with the problems of being in a celebrity relationship but it was even worse in this instance because nobody seemed to believe that it was for real! The relationship had only just started and it was being suffocated by all the cynicism and attention we were getting. At the time I decided that the best policy was to keep quiet. I didn't want to feed the media frenzy because it was threatening the relationship. Stories would appear with headlines about 'My Love for Chris' which were nonsense because I hadn't made any public comment. I felt (and still do) that the *detail* of our personal relationship was a private matter.

In the middle of all this madness, I found myself on the kids' TV show *Live & Kicking* one Saturday morning with Ronan Keating, who had left Boyzone by then to become a solo artist. We were sitting together on the sofa for the phone-in part of the programme when one of the presenters decided now would be the perfect time to ask me about Chris. It was a live show and I couldn't really refuse to answer so I just said, 'You say it best when you say nothing at all,' which was the name of Ronan's song at the time. The relationship was in a very early stage but it looked like something might be developing and I didn't want to jeopardise it by putting it under the spotlight in that way.

In the meantime, with the single about to be released, there was continuous promotional work to be done. It was relentless and the pressure to win the day was massive. It was so important to me to get to the top for a second time, because that felt like the difference between being a one-hit wonder and having a career. It seemed like I was spending every waking moment signing CDs at record stores, appearing on all the kids' TV shows, giving interviews to radio stations, newspapers and magazines and doing all I could to keep the momentum building.

Finally, on the Tuesday after its release, I got a call from EMI with the midweek chart position. I had been waiting nervously for the call because this was the first real indication of how the race was shaping up. I can't even remember who called me up that morning, but I do remember what they said. 'You're ahead, Geri, but only by two hundred copies.'

It was too close to call. All I could do was keep going. The rest of the week is a blur of record shops, autograph signing, media appearances and flash bulbs. I knew that I would get another chart position on the Friday and when it came I was delighted. I don't know if the original midweek position was a fluke but this time I was ahead by 30,000 copies! I was thrilled but I still didn't let myself slack off. I knew that Saturday was the busiest day in the shops and that it was crucial to stay visible right up to the last minute. On Saturday evening when it was all over I collapsed into bed and slept like a baby.

The next day was chart day. I was getting nervous waiting for the call, which I expected at around one or two o'clock, so Chris decided to take me for lunch to a health farm called Cliveden which is a beautiful stately home where the Profumo Affair started in the 1960s — they still have the swimming pool where Christine Keeler frolicked naked. I was trying to relax over lunch with Chris and forget about the charts when the call from EMI came through on my mobile. 'Lift Me Up' was the Number One single. It wasn't really the right place to go crazy but we ordered champagne and it was a fantastic moment to share. I had been scared that my career was on the skids after 'Look at Me' and *Schizophonic* but to have two consecutive solo Number One records under my belt was a brilliant feeling.

I had already decided that I wanted to have a big party on the Sunday evening, whatever the outcome. I just wanted to thank everyone who had helped now the whole thing was over. That night was the culmination of seven months' hard work and I was really in the mood to celebrate.

I wanted to have the party somewhere special, so I booked a reception room in a very grand private members' club called Home House in London which has beautiful marble staircases and wonderful art on the walls. I had food laid on and told everyone to order Krug champagne because I was picking up the bill! When Chris and I arrived at around eight o'clock, the party was already in full swing. The atmosphere was fantastic. As the champagne started to flow I got drunk pretty quickly and was going around the room egging everyone on to drink as much as they liked and really get into the party spirit. That was typical of me, I have never been someone who drinks every day. My attitude would be, if we are going to drink, let's get pissed! 'Come on everybody!' I was shouting, 'let's all get drunk together!' From there the night gets blurry. I think everybody left completely drunk. The next day I got an invoice for £30,000 — probably all my royalties from the record — and that was just the drinks bill! It was a lot of money but what is money for if not to enjoy an achievement like that?

I left the party early to make my way to Chris's house. I remember walking down the steps with my bodyguard Liam and seeing lots of paparazzi in the street. I was not at my best by then so Liam put me in the car with a coat over my head so they couldn't get a picture they could use. Liam left me in the car with my driver Calvin who drove me over to Chris's place. When we got there I was so drunk that I had trouble getting out of the car and I said to Calvin, 'Oh Calvin, I'm not sure I can walk.' Before I knew it, he had lifted me up over his shoulder and was carrying me from the car to the building. Then, sure enough, the paparazzi appeared and, drunk as I was, I could tell that this was one hell of a picture! My face was buried in Calvin's head, my hair was all over the place and I was clearly legless. I was saying, 'Calvin what are you doing? What are you doing?' but it was too late. By the time I was through the door they had their pictures.

The next day I surfaced quite early, dehydrated, shaking and with a splitting headache. This was the mother of all hangovers but I was determined to make it to the yoga class I had booked for that morning. As soon as I appeared, the paparazzi were onto me. They snapped away while I stood there with my little yoga mat squinting into the light, still feeling half-pissed. On the Tuesday morning the papers appeared and to my horror, there I was, off my face hoisted over Calvin's shoulder with my backside being paraded for the paparazzi! At the same time, I was feeling happy and secure enough to laugh it off as one of those things and not let it ruin my Tuesday. But my positive state of mind was to be short-lived. By Thursday my relationship with Chris Evans was over.

Chris and I were together for a month. It was a whirlwind and the ending came like a change in the weather. Suddenly, winter came and everything went cold. I can't explain why it happened that way because I don't know. There was a story in the papers that he had been seen kissing someone else and of course that was upsetting, but in the end, whether that was true or not, it was over.

The story about it all being a sham and the media attention didn't help our chances but I can't blame it all on external things because that's too easy. I have to take my part in it. Wherever the blame lay I had to move on and get on with it and I had to do it in public. I left for the MTV Awards in Dublin the next day, putting on a brave face, already knowing it was over.

It was too late for me to pull out of the award ceremony because I was due to present an award to Pierce Brosnan. I had been looking forward to the occasion and had had this gorgeous, show-stopping black dress made that looked great with my long curly blonde hair extensions. On the outside I was the golden girl celebrating her second Number One single, walking up the red carpet to a glamorous award ceremony to meet James Bond. Inside I was feeling like shit. None of the glitz or glamour seemed to matter.

I went through the evening on autopilot. Something clicked in, telling me that the show must go on. I suppose being a celebrity is just like any other job in that respect — you have to leave your problems at home. Throughout the day, I had found myself starting to eat sweets and chocolate just to keep me going. Sugar gives me a high and I was injecting myself with the drug of chocolates all day to stay up there. When a dip came, I'd put another one in my mouth to keep me on the plateau.

The whole evening was spent dodging questions about Chris and trying to keep my emotions in check. I smiled, I presented the award and I just tried to keep going but inside I was suffering badly. It was inevitable that people would ask me about Chris and I didn't know how to handle it. If most people had believed it was a publicity stunt before the split, everyone definitely would now it had ended so suddenly. It looked terrible but I thought that there was nothing I could do or say to make it better. I could only add petrol to the flames.

In the end I said 'it has nothing to do with me' to one reporter and that got picked up in the press. I suppose I was trying to detach myself from the whole PR scandal. I think I wanted to make it clear that as far as I was concerned, the relationship was real.

At the end of the night I went back to my hotel alone. I felt so empty. My make-up artist had made a big homemade lemon cake for me. It was covered in sugar and it was waiting for me in the room. I fooled myself that I was only going to have one slice. So I ate one, then another, then another and then another. Pretty soon it was all gone. I polished off the whole cake in one sitting.

On the Sunday morning I returned home. By then, the news had broken. I remember walking through the airport and seeing myself on the front covers of all the newspapers wearing my beautiful dress, with my mermaid hair, and the word DUMPED screaming at me from the headlines. One of them said something like 'How Could You Dump This Chris? Are You Mad?' and all I could think was — I am famous, blonde, rich, young and successful and I feel like I've got the word 'Dumped' stamped across my forehead.

In the car on the way home with the entourage who had come over to Dublin, my make-up artist and my hairdresser and others, we sat in silence. They had learned the news from the newsstands and none of them knew what to say to me. They had seen me a few weeks earlier so happy with Chris and now it was over. What could they say?

I sat there, my stomach in knots. Because of the media circus I decided to stay away from the whole big mess. It was the middle of November and the weather was cold and miserable. All there was left to do was to go back to my big empty house, lick my wounds and hide.

The Golden Cage

The curtains were drawn and they were going to stay that way — it didn't matter to me whether it was day or night anyway. The main source of light was the TV screen which flickered as Tony Soprano, in between appointments with his shrink, supervised another hit. I lay on the bed in my pyjamas and bath robe, only moving to reach out for the fix that kept me there — sugar.

A bag of sweets, chocolate bars, cakes and pastries lay by my side on the double bed. I could count my day as a success if I was able to replenish that supply and never really run out. The Tesco garage was a short drive away and open 24 hours, so they didn't care whether it was day or night either. It was a perfect arrangement.

I was a very different figure to the young woman in the show-stopping dress at the MTV Awards. It was mid-November and I couldn't face the world. Instead, I created one of my own at home in my bedroom at St Paul's. All of the hard work over the last year and the hype around 'Lift Me Up' had built to a crescendo over the previous few weeks and then sent me crashing back down. I was slipping fast from sadness into depression. I felt unable to express myself and I just felt it was more graceful and ladylike to assume a dignified silence as I had when I left the Spice Girls. The problem, as I have realised since then, is that suppressed feelings will manifest themselves in some other way. For me that meant bulimia, because bulimia is not about food, it's about not being heard.

I had everything I needed in my bedroom. This was the perfect opportunity to catch up on all the TV shows and movies I'd missed. I remember watching episode after episode of *The Sopranos*, killing the days by filling my head with the adventures of Tony, Carmela and Meadow. I just surrendered my days to the comforts of my big double bed. I had always hated the onset of winter anyway and I didn't think I was missing much by hiding from the November rain.

1999 had been relentless and I was exhausted after months of promotion. The balance sheet looked good after the two Number One singles and my solo career could now be counted as a real success but it had left me with nothing in reserve. A period of relaxation was what I needed but this was no recharging of the batteries. The warning signs about my eating disorders had been appearing since the 'Mi Chico Latino' video shoot but I was about to relapse severely.

Food was my drug. I would wake up in the morning and the first thing I would think about was what I was going to eat. My self-esteem was so low by that time that my other obsessions — limiting what I was eating and exercise — were taking a back seat. I had been so driven by the need to look thin that it was only a matter of time before I would swing completely the other way, and recent events had played their part in triggering it.

Once I started eating I couldn't stop. After a meal I'd find myself grazing on food. I'm bored. What shall I do? I'll eat.

I feel fat. What shall I do? Eat.

I'm feeling sad and lonely. What shall I do? I'll shove something in my mouth.

My response to any feeling was to eat because eating seemed to ease the feelings and take the edge off. Pretty soon it was habitual, non-stop eating.

I would stir myself once or twice a day or in the middle of the night, throw a sweatshirt and tracksuit bottoms over my pyjamas, put on a baseball cap and sunglasses, jump in the car and shoot off to the 24-hour Tesco and leave with a shopping bag full of supplies — cakes, chocolate bars and boxes of Celebrations. Sugary food has an extreme narcotic effect on me. It gives me a twenty-minute high followed by a dip into depression. I need a steady supply to keep me up. I felt like a drug addict venturing out to meet my dealer. The difference was that I couldn't get arrested for buying sweets or stopped for driving under the influence of chocolate. When I got home I went straight back to bed with the shopping bag and carried on eating.

My life became a permanent binge. I was becoming less of a bulimic and more of an overeater. I wasn't so concerned about expelling the food after eating but was keeping up a constant feeling of being full. Sometimes my back would hurt because my stomach was so full but I would carry on anyway until, eventually, I would pass out. Obviously I started to put on weight and that made me feel even worse.

Pretty soon everything else began to slip too. I would lie in the same pyjamas all day because I couldn't be bothered to change let alone get dressed and face the world. Every day is a bad hair day when you can't be bothered to wash it and mine was a greasy, tousled mess. I didn't look like a mermaid any more. I even stopped brushing my teeth. It was a cycle that seemed impossible to break.

The worse I felt about myself, the more I would just veg out in front of the TV and hide from the world.

St Paul's felt like it was miles from anywhere. I was 40 miles from Watford and an hour from London so it wasn't easy for people to just pop round to see me and I certainly wasn't in the mood to go visiting. I was distancing myself from people on purpose because I just felt so disgusting. I felt fat and ugly and I didn't want to be seen. It was self-perpetuating. I didn't like myself so I ate more.

In early December I was due to appear at the *Smash Hits* Awards. It was an important event which I would always try to attend but, as the day approached, I just couldn't face it. Part of the problem was that after lying in bed stuffing my face for three weeks, I couldn't fit into my clothes any more. I remember standing in my darkened bedroom, trying to psyche myself up for the ceremony and finding that I was just too big to force myself into the outfit I wanted to wear. I could hardly wear pyjamas to an awards ceremony so I called them up and cancelled.

I don't know if it was the *Smash Hits* cancellation that made me start to wake up but at some point I sensed that I was in a downward spiral and was drifting into very dangerous territory. It is difficult to describe the feelings I had. I didn't want to live but I didn't want to die either. I just wanted to be blank and let the world go by. I had even started to take Diazepam tranquillisers so I could sleep for fifteen hours at a time.

As December wore on, I began to realise that things had gone too far. Deep down, I have an instinct for self-preservation that seems to kick in before things reach the point of no return. I could feel myself drowning in depression and knew I had to reach for something to keep me afloat. Typically, the factor that made a difference was my weight.

I had my own gym at the house and I began to force myself out of bed to use it. I was only motivated by a desire to work off the weight I was gaining but, whatever the reason, it was a positive step to get out of bed and do anything at all. Gradually my old obsessive tendencies started to reassert themselves and I began exercising for three hours at a time. I was overcompensating, running for hours, but at least I was coming alive again.

I also had to finish off *Geri's World Walkabout*. The majority of work on the programme had already been done but I still had to film the pieces that would link the film together and the trailers that the BBC needed to promote the programme. The plan was that we would go on a special trip to South Africa so that we could do the filming somewhere suitably exotic and sunny.

The director, David Green, came over to the house that December. I had been dreading the trip to Africa but being the executive producer, I felt very committed to the project. Despite that, I had to tell David that I just couldn't face getting on another plane having done in excess of 150 flights already that year. I felt really bad about letting him down but there was just no way. I didn't even want to leave my house let alone fly halfway round the world.

We had to find a compromise. By then, I was at least going on walks in the garden, so I suggested that we do the filming there. It wasn't ideal but in the end he had no choice. I wore a big brown coat and had a puffy face which I tried to mask by overcompensating with my hair and make-up. I looked like something out of *Dallas* or *Knots Landing* freezing in the December chill in front of my oversized dream house in the country, with big hair and over-the-top lip-gloss. I was a million miles from the excited and lively character that featured in the rest of the show. The whole thing seemed strained and artificial and, proud as I am of the rest of the programme, that part made me cringe.

The important thing, though, was that I had achieved something more than making it to Tesco and back for the first time in weeks. Even though I had been in a really black hole there was a little piece inside of me that wouldn't give up. I had turned the sound down from life for a while but gradually I was starting to emerge and reach out again. I started making dates for a yoga lesson or setting a time to meet some friends. Finally, I could see a tiny pinprick of light at the end of the tunnel.

I always saw St Paul's as a diamond in the middle of a muddy puddle. There was the nunnery next door and a few houses across the road but it was easy to feel alone there. Friends and family did spend time visiting and staying over but the only regular company I had were Mary and Larry, my housekeepers. The house had so many nooks and crannies that it could be pretty spooky and I would whip myself into a frenzy if I let it get to me.

I had a state-of-the-art security system installed, with razor wire on the perimeter and a laser beam to pick up anyone who came over the fence. Sometimes I felt like a canary trapped in a beautiful golden cage, living in luxury but locked in by the same bars that were there to keep others out. Such fears weren't just the product of an overactive imagination. I had become very security aware because I had reason to be. Fame is a magnet for a wide variety of misfits and unbalanced people.

One morning at nine o'clock the doorbell rang. Mary answered the door and I listened in on the intercom. I could hear a man's voice saying that he wanted to do disgusting things to me, and poor Mary had to deal with it, telling him to leave and threatening to call the police. It was frightening knowing there was someone like that just a few yards away outside the gates.

There was another guy who would stand outside the house for hours on end. He just stared up at the windows or tried to peer into the car when I drove out. I felt as if I was continually burdened with these nutters and it was driving me into a state of fear. In the end I decided to beef up the protection just to be on the safe side.

There was another man who kept calling my record company and Freuds the PR company and complaining that they weren't looking after me properly or managing my career in the right way. He would also write to them, using the name Mr Sand, and claim that he was my rightful manager. The letters and phone calls got worse as time went on and in the end he called Freuds claiming he had planted a bomb there. He was obviously obsessed and it was terrifying. I was getting more and more scared and started to convince myself that someone was out to get me.

Someone had already set off the alarm by climbing over the fence earlier in the year but then, one night that winter, the alarm inside the house went off late at night. I was locked away in my bedroom but I got up and went to listen at the door. I could hear someone creeping up the stairs. I was only wearing my knickers and bra and I was terrified. I had panic buttons in the bedroom, which I pressed, but I had no idea what else to do. I climbed back onto the bed, holding my Ivor Novello award to use as a weapon, paralysed with fear. After what seemed like an age, the door opened — it was Mary checking to see I was OK and making sure that nobody had got to me.

As it turned out, there was no intruder, or none that we could find. Something had triggered the alarm but we never found out what or who it had been.

One morning I was up in my bedroom watching TV when Mary came upstairs as usual to bring me my post. I lay on the bed, going through the letters with one eye while watching TV with the other. Eventually, I came to a small white envelope addressed in biro to 'Miss G Halliwell'. Must be from a fan, I thought, opening it and removing a piece of folded A4 paper. When I saw what was inside,

Millennium party!

hiding in the library

Max, Nat, & me!

Cruiser lift me up

Christmas 1999
I used this table twice.

July 1999 St Tropez

My beautiful nephews.

Hotel du Lap
fantastic Thursday for
family bonding

ooh charles you look
dashing

Somewhere in Germany
doing promos.

Harry and me by the sea
day after the G.AY.gig.

Mothers wedding.
Spring 1999

Venice Promo for
for 16 rang men.

VENICE LOOK NOW DOWN!!
JENIE 4

LEAVING VENICE.
PARIS + DEZON SPEEDING TO THE AIRPORT my best maid.

Big Happy Bikini
Buyer!

exhausted!

lionel richie
nicest guy
in the biz

LIONEL GERI
+ MIC

25 June 2001
milan Miguel ugung

Miguel my
No1 dancer!

C'MON UP N
C ME SOME TIME.

"All By myself!"

Bridget Jones
Impressia

Day off in
Canada
My little pony

BARBIE AND
HER PONY

DAY OFF MAY
2007.

lucky black cat

Met the Girls May 2001

Robbie Huey + me playing house.

Sabrina Robbie + me Zimbabwe.

Yoga can be done anywhere even on safari.

The only way to travel on a freebie on some rich guy's jet!

Me with my new best friend Nellie the elephant.

I froze. The photocopied piece of paper looked like a ransom note in a kidnap case, the letters cut out from newspapers, spelling the words:

WE WILL KILL YOU GAY LOVER
YOU FUCKING BITCH. WE WILL KILL YOU

At the bottom of the note were the words Combat 18 — the right-wing terror group. The threat seemed to be linked to my relationship with George and my support for gay rights and it came only six months after the murder of three people by a nail bomber in a gay pub in Soho. I lay on the bed reading the ugly words over and over. I reached for the phone and called my security man Liam.

'Hello?'

'It's Geri.'

'Hi, Geri. How are you?'

'Please come over to the house. Now.'

The murder of Jill Dando had made it impossible for celebrities to laugh off these sorts of threats and the gay angle fitted in with the new homophobic focus of right-wing groups. I lay there terrified until Liam arrived and took a look at the letter.

'I'll deal with this now, Geri,' he said. 'It's probably some nutter playing a prank but I'll let the police know. You should just try not to worry about it. You are safe here.'

In a strange way, I think my unhappy and zombie-like state of mind saved me from going crazy with worry. I felt safer in St Paul's with the high-tech security system than anywhere else and my bingeing seemed to insulate me from the worse feelings of fear. Then I got a call from the police who told me they would like to send someone down to discuss the matter. A few days later an officer from Scotland Yard reassured me over a cup of tea that no one would kill me but said that they took all such threats seriously and would monitor the situation. In the meantime, I should be careful and let them know as soon as anything similar arrived. As he was leaving he turned to me and said, 'Oh, and if you do get anything else like that in the post, just be careful and try to avoid getting fingerprints on it.' I felt a little better having involved the police and decided that the only thing I could do was put the fear at the back of my mind and not let the people who sent out such poison win.

As Christmas approached, I was desperate to find a way to shake myself out of my destructive frame of mind. Typically, though, I looked to external solutions rather than inward at the roots of my unhappiness. A frequent strategy was something I call a 'geographic'. The thinking behind a geographic is pretty straightforward — if you can't change the way you feel, then change where you are when you are feeling it. In other words, when in pain, go on holiday because a change in location might just do the trick.

One Sunday at about seven o'clock I phoned my friend Linda.

'Do you want to go away somewhere?' I asked.

'Um, OK. When? Where?' she said.

'What about skiing? Let's book it tonight and go tomorrow. What do you think?' I asked, by now getting excited.

'Oh. So soon?'

'Yeah, Come on.'

And Linda, being Linda, said yes. So that's what we did. We booked a flight to Whistler, a ski-resort in Canada, and jumped onto an aeroplane the next day. I think it was the idea more than the reality that appealed to me because it meant I had to force myself out of bed and get organised quickly. It also meant a serious shock to the system. I went from weeks of inactivity and overdosing on sugar in the comfort of my bedroom to a ten-hour flight to Canada which I planned to follow with a week's exertions on the piste. As soon as I boarded the aircraft, I realised I had made a mistake. I was exhausted. My body was coming down from the sugar and I felt washed out and lethargic.

Once we got to the resort I just felt worse. It was freezing cold and the last thing I was up to was lugging around heavy skis while wearing enormous ski boots. I immediately felt absolutely drained and abandoned any idea of skiing. Linda was having a great time, so I left her to enjoy the slopes and holed up in the hotel, having a few massages but feeling physically ill and run down. After three days I went to Linda's room to tell her that I really wanted to go home and we caught the next plane back to Britain. The thing about a geographic is that you take the same 'you' with you when you go. I thought I could change myself by altering my location but it was madness. It had changed nothing.

When I got back to St Paul's I realised how foolish the idea had been. I remember going upstairs to my familiar room and saying to myself, 'You really have to pull yourself out of this now, Geri.' A few days later I called my record company and arranged an early Christmas meal for all the people there who had worked so hard for me. I hadn't seen these people since the party to celebrate 'Lift Me Up' going to Number One and I am sure they were shocked by the way I'd changed in the six weeks since. The girl with the champagne tab, the Number One single and the brand new relationship had been replaced by someone in a cocoon of bingeing and depression. I was catatonic, hardly able to string a sentence together, but if anyone noticed they didn't say.

As Christmas got closer I had to think about how to handle the festive season. For a bulimic over-eater it is a time of great temptation and pressure. Ironically, the plans I made for the Christmas and New Year of 1999 seemed to shake me out of my depression and broke the cycle of bingeing. Eating disorders are usually played out in secret. I would not binge in front of my family or friends and that saved me in the end.

The first part of the plan was inviting Mum and her boyfriend Steve and my brother and sisters and their families to spend the day with me at St Paul's. The second was the decision to host an enormous New Year's Eve party to celebrate the Millennium. I decided that the house had been full of depression and negativity for too long and that the best way to change that was to throw a party and to make it huge.

The family Christmas and Millennium party became my new focus. Rather than leave all the work to my housekeepers, I listened to my mum's advice and took a course in occupational therapy — cleaning and polishing and hoovering the house from top to bottom. Mum thought I'd allowed myself to be mollycoddled too long and that I needed to take some responsibility for myself and some pride in my home. So I got down on my knees and scrubbed the skirting boards and polished the silver. Mum was right — it felt great and I could feel the depression beginning to lift.

I'm not known for doing anything by half-measures so for the Millennium party I drew up a long guest list of friends and family from school days to the present and sent out invitations. Everyone wants to spend the New Year with their loved ones so I thought I'd really go for it and told everyone on the list that they could bring five other people just as long as they told me the names in advance. That way everyone was happy and I had an enormous party on my hands.

The prospect of an action-packed Christmas and New Year with Geri playing hostess also jolted me out of my bingeing. By the time Christmas arrived I was back to my 'healthy' regime, cutting out fats and carbohydrates and controlling my calories. I was also doing serious time in the gym. I wanted to look as good as I could for the big party and it felt good to regain control. My family came over on Christmas Day and we christened my long dining table with a full Christmas meal. There I was, after six weeks of bingeing alone in my bedroom, eating Christmas dinner with my family, cutting back on my portions and skipping the roast potatoes and mince pies. Squeaky-clean Geri was back, just in time for the annual Christmas pig-out!

Around this time, Mum and Steve announced to the family that they planned to marry the following May. Mum had met Steve eight years earlier when they both worked at the Harlequin shopping centre in Watford — Mum as a cleaner and Steve as an electrician — and I had always got on very well with him. Even so, when she told me they were marrying I felt like a little girl again. Somehow, I began to feel the loss of my dead father.

Millennium Eve started a little strangely. The house was overrun with people I didn't know, getting the place ready. There were caterers there and people putting up balloons and laying out the chairs and setting the tables. I went into the kitchen and saw my mum in there and, on the other side of the room, this big fat man at the table. I didn't recognise him so I asked Mum if she knew who he was. She wasn't sure but had assumed he was a security man. He looked too out of shape for a security man to me so I went over and asked politely who he was. He looked up very calmly and said he was a security man and that he'd been sent to keep an eye on things by Mr Sand. I couldn't believe it. Here he was saying that the man who had been making threatening phone calls to my PR company, had sent him to my house and he had got into my kitchen completely unchallenged. I told this man that Mr Sand was some oddball who kept pretending to represent me and that he'd been misled.

I asked for his number and told him I'd speak to the police about it in the New Year and so, with me apologising profusely, he left. It seems so obvious now to me, but it wasn't until I described the incident and the man to the police that I realised that the man sitting at my kitchen table was Mr Sand himself. Later that Millennium Eve night, George Harrison was attacked in his own house in Oxfordshire.

I didn't have time to dwell on the incident because I had to put the finishing touches to the house. I was so proud of how beautiful it looked. I needed to compose myself because I still wasn't completely recovered from the previous six weeks of illness and depression. I had been neglecting my yoga but I did some that evening because I knew it would calm me down. I was very excited but, as usual, I was worried that nobody would show up. The invites said to arrive from eight o'clock so I decided to go upstairs and watch *EastEnders* and then go down and see if anyone was there by half past.

Upstairs, as I watched the goings-on in Albert Square, I got ready for the party. I wore a long black skirt and a pretty pink cardigan and had my hair done. When I looked in my bedroom mirror I got a real lift. I felt prettier than I had in a long time. So, once *EastEnders* was over, I decided to take a look to see how the party was going and greet any guests that might have arrived.

I remember walking down my first staircase, which is on the third floor, and hearing noise from down below. By the time I reached the second floor I could not move for people. It was like walking into a club; the house was rocking. There were so many people that it was hard to focus on one person. I probably knew two thirds and the rest were their friends and family. My mum's friends were there and there were kids, grandmas and, of course, celebrities.

There was such a variety of people from so many aspects of my life, all meeting in one huge celebration. There were Watford people and current friends like George and Kenny and Dawn and Lenny. Des O'Connor and his wife were there and Dane Bowers from Another Level with his girlfriend of the time Jordan, and I remember seeing Martin Kemp and his wife Shirley from Wham! There was one girl from my old school days who was very pissed and kept on coming up to me, looking at me very seriously and saying, 'I'm not after your money, Geri. I'm not after your money.'

It was an extraordinary cross-section of people and they were all getting on fine and mixing brilliantly. It was so odd seeing members of my family and old friends from school getting down on the dance floor and shaking their stuff with Des O'Connor and Jordan. It was all pretty random but it seemed to work. Even a couple of the nuns from next door showed up and had a dance.

The best part came at midnight when we had an amazing firework display. I had spent a small fortune on it but I didn't expect it to be so spectacular. I remember standing outside with everyone, having a great time, feeling really pleased with myself that it had all worked out so well. Inside, the place was still jumping and I could tell the house was getting trashed. In the end, though, even I was stubbing my cigarettes out on the floor because it didn't seem to matter. I felt like the negative vibes had been well and truly banished.

The next morning was like that old Yellow Pages advert, the morning after the night before. I kept finding people sleeping under coats at ten o'clock in the morning and asking, 'Who are you?'. Amazingly, only a soap dish and one tiny photo frame got broken, which wasn't bad considering the hundreds of guests. There were fags and drinks everywhere but as I surveyed the wreckage that morning, it felt well worth it. It really lifted my spirits. It was time for some optimism for the 21st century.

It was to be a busy New Year for me. I had 'Bag It Up' planned as the fourth single from the album and was booked to appear at the Brits in March. The first thing I had to do was work on a concept for the video and start thinking about the routine and set for the Brits performance.

I sometimes think the saga of Geri and the Spice Girls is like one of those old movies — just when you think our plucky heroine has escaped, the Spice Monster rises from the dead to pursue her once more. It didn't matter how many times I shot Ginger, she just refused to die.

Aprilia were an Italian scooter manufacturer who had signed a deal to sponsor the Spice Girls' world tour while I was still a member of the group. They had designed a limited edition set of Spice Sonic scooters featuring the images of the five girls. When I left, the company refused to pay all of the advance due to the Spice Girls. The girls sued Aprilia for the money and they counter-claimed, saying my departure made the Spice Sonic bikes a marketing disaster. They also said that the other girls must have already known I was planning to leave when the deal was signed. The girls asked me to go to the High Court in London to testify on their behalf.

The case was a matter between the company and the Spice Girls but I felt that I owed it to them to go to court and try to help, if that was what they wanted. It wasn't an easy thing to do because the case centred on the consequences for the group by me leaving. I wasn't proud of the timing of my departure and everyone had been very worried it would harm ticket sales on the world tour and involve the band in legal action. Thankfully, with the exception of this case, those fears had proved unfounded.

It was a cold February day and I was dressed in my most sober black trouser suit. The car pulled up outside the High Court and, as I got out, I was immediately surrounded by paparazzi. I suppose I should have been used to that sort of attention but it felt unfamiliar after months of hibernation. I was able to smile and appear unflustered but inside I was dreading the prospect of appearing before a court and raking over the past.

Ever since I was a little girl, I have been good at putting on an act and covering up my true feelings and that was exactly what was required in the solemn atmosphere of the wood-panelled courtroom. As I looked up at the witness box and the judge, The Honourable Mrs Justice Arden, I took a deep breath and told myself to relax and tell the truth. But once I was up there, I felt like a five-year-old again, under the gaze of the headmistress, stupid and scared. I was desperate to tell the truth but wanted to make sure I said nothing to hurt the girls' case.

The lawyer acting for the scooter company, Andrew Sutcliffe, wanted to prove that the girls and I already knew when the deal was signed that five would become four. The problem was that I couldn't remember very clearly the details he was asking me about. He then turned to the timing of my decision to leave and asked me exactly when I had let the others know.

'I was drip-feeding the idea to the others as well as myself,' I told him, worried he was trying to catch me out in some way. 'That's why there wasn't any defining moment when I can say I consciously made that decision. It was like leaving a marriage, you get such mixed feelings. One part of me wanted to stay but the other half said it was time to go.' And that was the truth.

The newspapers were full of reports and pictures the next day saying I had seemed confident and relaxed and smiling in the witness box. Inside, I was struggling to hide how difficult it was. Two weeks later, the girls lost the case and a lot of money which I was really sorry about but at least I could say I'd done my bit.

The Brit Awards followed shortly after the trial, guaranteeing that speculation about my relationship with the Spice Girls would stay on the front pages. The girls had been concentrating on their solo careers and families during 1999 but the organisers of the Brits had persuaded them to return for the 2000 show. The prospect of performing on the same bill as the girls was daunting enough but the awards committee were about to raise the stakes. They wanted to give the Spice Girls an 'Outstanding Contribution to the British Music Industry' Award and they wanted me to collect it with them.

The show was already a big deal for me because the Brits have a special place in my heart. The 1997 show where I had worn Ginger's famous Union Jack dress had been the high point of Spice world domination. Now, three years later, I wanted to make an impact as a solo artist and didn't want the event dominated by talk about the Spice Girls and Geri and their award. It was an honour to be offered the opportunity to accept my share of it and I was pleased that the Brits hadn't forgotten the importance of my role in the success of the band, but I was uncomfortable with the idea from the start.

Anyway, getting an Outstanding Contribution Award is a bit like getting a gold watch when you are retiring and I wasn't ready for that. The Spice Girls were going to the Brits to show they were still around and I was there to promote my solo career. It was too soon to think about reunions and this was not the time for nineties nostalgia! And so I said, 'Thanks, but no.'

There were also personal reasons to turn down the award. I hadn't had the chance in the two years since I left to enjoy a private reunion with the girls, so it felt wrong to set one up for the TV cameras. I wanted to see them away from the glare of publicity, but the powers that be seemed to be trying to manipulate us and push us together for a moment that we weren't ready for. I don't really blame them for asking because it would've made great television but it wasn't right for the girls and it wasn't right for me.

The Brits was scheduled for 3rd March at Earl's Court and, award or no award, it was clearly going to be a big night for me. I had planned a performance of 'Bag It Up' that was going to be the most ambitious production number I had ever attempted. At the same time, the distraction of the Spice Girls award was being built up by the media into some sort of showdown.

On top of that there was another far more serious and sinister development. Another threatening letter had just arrived.

YOU FUCKING SLAG
GAY LOVER
BRITS — YOU WILL DIE

Below the message there was my photograph and next to that three bullets cut out from a newspaper appearing to enter my head. As I stared at the piece of paper, the terror I had been suppressing began to boil up inside me. This time the threat was very clear and very real. They said they were going to shoot me and Brits 2000 was to be the night.

As usual I was starving myself in preparation for the event, having learned nothing from my miserable autumn in St Paul's. The video shoot for 'Bag It Up' was a perfect example. I had been on the Dr Atkins diet and seemed to be living on slices of turkey and little else but that wasn't enough. In the final days before the video shoot, I started a three-day fast of maple syrup and water because I was so desperate to lose some more weight. I learned to live through the crippling hunger pains and feelings of overpowering weakness that came with this regime because I wanted so badly to be thin. *Just a few more days to go until the shoot. Keep going, Geri, it's the only way to be thin enough.* It was madness because a binge was always around the corner. I was in a hotel in Italy a day or so before the video shoot when I woke up in the middle of the night with hunger pains so severe that I couldn't hold out. My body had had enough and woken me up screaming: 'Eat!' I obeyed, clambering out of my bedclothes to the mini-bar where I ate all the cookies I could find. No wonder — I was literally starving.

The shoot itself was gruelling. The video required me to learn to tap dance and I had to perfect an exhausting pole-dance routine which left me with bruises on my knees, but I was very happy with the final product. I was also reasonably happy with the way I looked — despite the cookies — but with Brits night approaching there was no room for slacking on the starvation diet. Just let me get through the next thing, I thought, and then everything will be OK.

The most important thing at an event like the Brits is making an impact. That was always how it had been with the Spice Girls and I wanted to prove I could do it on my own. It made no difference who else was on the bill, I wanted my performance to be the best. My former band mates' presence may have added an extra edge to the situation but it wasn't my motivation. This was about the future, not the past.

Luca called round to see me one morning early in the year to discuss the Brits performance. I wanted something that would fit in with the gender issues in the video and the song and which would take the idea one step further. Luca said he had an idea and I couldn't wait to hear about it.

'Why don't you arrive on stage from between a pair of enormous legs?' he said.

'A pair of legs?'

'Yes.'

'You think I should appear from *between* them?'

'That's right. And I think you should be pole-dancing like in the video.'

'So, basically, you are saying you think I should arrive on stage pole-dancing out of an enormous crotch?'

'Yes.'

'Oh my God, Luca! Are you *joking*?'

But he wasn't. It seemed shocking at first but then, as I thought about it, I started to giggle and realised how brilliant an idea it was. It seemed appropriate that as the most famous advocate of Girl Power I should emerge on stage from between a pair of enormous female legs. It was funny and provocative — Geri's rebirth at the Brits. Perfect.

The death threats kept coming in the weeks running up to the Brits. At first, I was terrified. The threat seemed so real and so specific that, for a short time, I considered going public about it or maybe even pulling out of the evening. I had spoken to the police again about the situation and they tried to put my mind at rest. They reassured me that they were taking it seriously and that security at the event would be tight. I was frightened but in the end, the only way I was able to deal with it was to disassociate myself from the whole thing and pretend it wasn't happening. I didn't want to give in to the sick people who had sent the letters, so I vowed to go ahead. As the pressure grew it even occurred to me that with all I had to worry about, it might just be simpler if I was shot — it would be the perfect excuse if anything went wrong!

During rehearsals in the run-up to the show, I admit it didn't help my nerves to know that my former band mates might be watching me fluff the words or get the routine wrong. It was like performing in front of your old school buddies. It's far more nerve-wracking because you care what they think more than anyone else.

It was a complicated routine and I spent a long time working on the choreography, the set and my look. I planned to rip off my shirt at the start of the show to reveal a Union Jack bra I had had made especially for the performance. It was fun to play with the history of the Spice Girls and send myself up at the same time and I thought a Union Jack bra would do the trick. I was very excited when the bra arrived at St Paul's and hurried to the mirror to see how I looked. The problem was that no matter what angle I viewed myself from, the new bra made my boobs look bigger than they really were.

They seemed to scream 'Tits!' and I was sure they would draw too much attention. It was all very well to play with my images from the past but this was going too far — Ginger was one thing but this was Bet Lynch. In the end I ditched the bra in favour of a black one and a tiny Union Jack on my belt.

On the final day of rehearsals at Earl's Court, my nerves were building. I was convinced that something would go wrong. The trickiest part was when I had to walk along the backs of my team of dancers in high-heeled boots! I was so frightened that I would slip off. It was getting towards the end of my allotted time on stage and the Brits crew were getting impatient. We had done the routine so many times but when Luca said, 'OK Geri, I think we have it,' I insisted we give it one last try. Everything went smoothly until I started to walk along the boys' backs, at which point the heel of my left boot snapped and I fell on my backside. It didn't help my nerves but I was so relieved that I'd done that extra rehearsal, otherwise the heel would have snapped during the performance and taken my career with it.

The music had started but all I could hear was screaming. At first the noise was coming from beyond the stage in the pit where the real fans at the Brits 2000 were squashed together, their excitement building as, over the opening chunky, funky bars of 'Bag It Up' a voice proclaimed:

'Laaay-dees and Gentlemen! Miss. Geri. HALLI-WELLLLL!!!!'

The next screams were mine. As I stood in the wings breathing rapidly, on the verge of panic, the weeks of preparation, fear and expectation came together and crashed into this one moment.

Here. Now.

I clung on to Luca for support as the nerves took control of my body and I started to shake.

'Oh my God, Luca. I don't think I can do this.'

'Come on, Geri. Listen to the crowd. They want to see you. This is it. You need to let go of the tension and get out there.'

'I can't, Luca,' I said, looking up at him. 'I can't even move.'

'Scream,' he said, staring straight back. 'Let it all out. Then get out there because time is running out. Come on, Geri! Scream!'

So I grasped Luca, closed my eyes and screamed at the top of my lungs. As I did I could feel the tension start to ease. A second later, I was swept up from the side of the stage by my crew and hoisted onto an enormous lap-dancing pole. I still couldn't see the crowd but I knew my moment was coming and I could feel the adrenalin rushing through my body. Then the bass kicked in and 'Bag It Up' was in full flow. *Here we go*. The crowd erupted as I came into view, high up on the pole, descending to join my team of sixteen dancers on the biggest vagina in rock 'n' roll history and singing the opening lines:

'I like chocolate and controversy

He likes Fridays and bad company'

I looked out at the crowd and noticed that the music-industry types who made up the majority of the crowd had looked up from their chicken satay and put down their glasses of champagne. It seemed I had got their attention.

The high of performance is the greatest I have ever experienced. I was scared but exhilarated. The routine felt like an assault course. As I walked across the backs of my dancers I told myself to grip onto each guy as hard as I could. I was dreading losing my balance and falling into the throng of bodies. Gradually, I felt my nerves easing a little and began to enjoy it more. The positive reaction of the crowd was sending the adrenalin pumping through my body but I couldn't relax for a second. I was getting closer to the end and, as I was lifted up into the air for the final time, I said to myself, *Nearly there, Geri, just one more little thing to do*. I looked out at the crowd and pulled my arms back in a salute as the music died and the crowd exploded. A voice inside my head said one word over and over, *Yes, Yes, Yes*. I had done it and the relief was enormous. Nobody had tried to shoot me, I hadn't fallen over and I had gone down well. I was ecstatic.

I ran off stage and rushed back to my dressing room to change. My family had a table in the auditorium and I wanted to go and say hello. As I walked out into the main hall and crossed the room, I was still glowing from the success of the performance and I couldn't wait to share my happiness with my mum and the rest of the family. Mum looked really proud and I sat down at the table to have a drink with them all. But, before I knew it, I could hear the hostess Davina McCall announcing that it was time for the Outstanding Contribution to the Music Industry Award. The Spice Girls were about to hit the stage. Then, as Davina recounted the girls' successes, a chant grew from the front of the stage. It took me a while to work out what it was, but then I realised. They were chanting 'Geri, Geri'.

It was a bittersweet moment for me. It was wonderful to know what the fans felt and I was so grateful for the credit they felt I deserved but, at the same time, it brought home the sadness of the situation. My old friends were about to burst on stage to sing the songs that we wrote together and to celebrate the career I built with them. I could feel the memories flooding back and realised how much I missed them all. As I looked around the room, I could see the eyes of all of those around me searching my face for a sign of the emotions welling up inside, but I wasn't ready to cry or come up with a smile to cover my feelings. It was all too much. Part of me wanted to see them perform and enjoy the show but this was their moment, not mine, so I decided it was time to leave. I said goodbye to the table and apologised as the opening bars of 'Spice Up Your Life' began and I rushed out of the building as quickly as I could.

I returned to Home House, the beautiful hotel nearby where I had celebrated 'Lift Me Up' reaching Number One. I went upstairs to my room where Harry was waiting for me, yapping at the door. I was so high from the performance and emotional from the award episode that I just wanted to collapse on my bed for a while and then — as the high dipped and the emotion grew — I called room service. My emotions and my cravings, after weeks of controlling, demanded chocolate cake. I felt I had earned it.

After I had eaten I just wanted to go to sleep. Apart from anything else, I had to do a morning TV show the next day and needed to rest. The place was quite noisy because a post-Brits party was in full swing on the floor below but I was so exhausted I was sure I could sleep anyway. I got undressed down to my bra and knickers and was about to get into bed when I noticed the room-service tray, the incriminating evidence of my binge. There was no way I was leaving that in the room to find in the morning so I got up to put it outside in the corridor. As I opened the door, Harry, seeing a chance to explore, sped past me out into the hallway.

Instinctively I went to go after him and as I did the bedroom door thudded shut behind me.

I didn't know what to do. I was stranded in the hallway in my bra and knickers with no way to get anyone's attention, unless, that is, I was willing to go downstairs to the party which was packed with press, music-industry people and celebrities including Tom Jones and of all people, Chris Evans. Faced with the choice I preferred to sit it out on the corridor floor with Harry and a tray of dirty chocolate cake dishes. Eventually, I spotted a member of staff and called him over for help. I don't know how he stopped himself from laughing but I have him to thank for letting me in and then keeping my humiliation quiet.

Whoever you are, thank you — you were the complete professional. You rescued me on what was one of the most triumphant, traumatic and ridiculous nights of my life.

Heaven and Hell

I was tucked inside a rucksack, curled into a tiny ball, my knees pulled up tight under my chin. With no room to move, I was struggling to breathe in the enclosed space. I remember thinking that this is how it must feel to be a kidnap victim, bundled into darkness, disoriented and carried off by your captors. But I was a willing prisoner and my heart was beating fast with the exhilaration of the moment. I'd played a lot of games with my new friends that summer but this was easily the best.

'You ready, Geri?' Jonny said.

'Yeah,' I said, my voice muffled, 'let's go.'

I could hear the others walking ahead and opening the door and then felt myself being lifted up and carried out after them into the summer night. Ahead of me, I could hear voices and the clicking of cameras.

'Robbie, come on, mate, give us a picture.'

'Ere Robbie, where's Geri, then?'

I could imagine the scene. The usual paparazzi would be there, camped outside Robbie Williams' house in west London waiting to get THE picture. Rumours had been flying around for weeks that Rob and I were friends. A picture of us leaving his home in the early hours of the morning would be confirmation of that and more. In the eyes of the paparazzi and the tabloid editors it would be evidence of the best tabloid scoop of all — celebrity romance.

Sometimes fame makes your life feel like a game. The challenge involves protecting yourself from those who make a living from capturing your image or finding out private information about you. At the same time, being a singer or a movie star or a politician means that sometimes you need to work with the very people you spend the rest of your life trying to avoid. You need them to get your music or movie known or your message across and once you've done that you can't just politely ask them to leave you alone. That's not how the game is played.

Curled up inside that rucksack I felt the thrill of winning a round in the fame game. It was a delicious risk too because if it had given way and I had fallen out, sprawling onto the road under the noses of the paparazzi, they would have got the picture of the year and I would have suffered more than an invasion of privacy. How much dignity would a girl have left after falling out of a bag onto her arse in the street?

I was lucky to escape that humiliation and felt a wave of elation and relief as the photographers' voices faded.

'Nearly there, Geri. Rob's gone ahead in your Aston,' whispered Jonny, Rob's best friend, who must have been feeling the strain himself by now. 'I'll just put you down while I open the car door.' I waited as he opened the back door of Rob's Range Rover and then felt myself lifted up and deposited onto the back seat. As the car pulled away I lifted my head and peeked out of the top of the rucksack and then, when we were safely away, whooped and screamed with laughter, overcome with the sheer joy of the triumph. We had beaten the paparazzi at their own game of hide and seek and my friendship with Rob was still our secret. At least for now.

My performance at the Brits had inspired some hysterical headlines. *The Daily Mail* called me the QUEEN OF SLEAZE and devoted a whole page to the story. They said I had 'scaled new heights of offensiveness' with a 'mime so sleazy that it shocked even music-industry figures'. I had to laugh because it was so ridiculous. *Oh come on*, I thought, when asked about it by the press. 'This is rock 'n' roll,' I said, 'not a public service announcement.' I didn't really mind about the coverage because I didn't think anybody in the real world would see it as anything other than a bit of fun and I don't mind a bit of controversy. Without a little outrage the world would be a boring place. Anyway, I had a single to promote and I didn't think the attention would do me any harm. If I wasn't seen as a solo star before the Brits, I certainly was afterwards!

After the pressures of the earlier months of the year I was looking forward to taking a break, but after the unhappiness of the previous autumn I wanted to make sure that I was somewhere supportive and safe. I didn't want to leave myself isolated in St Paul's again. I decided to give George and Kenny a call and see what they were up to, hoping we might be able to hook up at their home in Los Angeles. It turned out that George was going to be busy in the studio for a while but Kenny was around, so we decided to have some relaxation time together. I was pretty confident that 'Bag It Up' was going to do well and it became clear as the Sunday chart approached that I was on course for a third solo Number One and without the usual nail-biting finish. It was wonderful to achieve it again and I have to admit that I took some pleasure in proving my critics wrong. *Schizophonic* had given me four hit singles — three of them Number Ones. I was on a high as I got on the plane to California.

George and Kenny have a beautiful house in Los Angeles with a wonderful sun deck and swimming pool and for the first few days, while George worked, Kenny and I just hung out and sunbathed. With the exhilaration of promotional work over I felt as if everything had suddenly stopped and gone silent and I knew I would be left alone with myself and the lurking danger of slipping suddenly into depression and bingeing, so it was such a relief to be able to spend time with Kenny to save me from that. We spent our time lying in the sun, shopping at the Beverly Centre or on Melrose Avenue or just going for long runs. One night, we watched the movie *Thelma and Louise*.

'I would love to do that,' I said. 'Just pack my bags and disappear for a while.'

'Well, why don't we?' said Kenny. 'We can go tomorrow morning in the convertible and just drive up the coast to San Francisco.'

It was such an exciting idea to do something so spontaneous. Usually, every move is mapped out for me and planned weeks or months in advance. So, the next morning we jumped into Kenny's

Mercedes convertible and set off up the Pacific Coast Highway towards San Francisco. The highway winds its way up the coast of California and the rocky coastline and crashing waves of the Pacific Ocean provide spectacular scenery. Inspired by the film, Kenny and I took on the personalities and accents of a couple of white trash from America's Deep South. I called myself Jodely and Kenny named himself Bubba. All the way up the coast we tried to stay in character and when we stopped for food or petrol, we would really play it up. As a Texan, Kenny's accent didn't raise too many eyebrows, but mine was less convincing. We stopped at one store where there was a little old lady behind the counter and I thought I would give the voice a try with her.

'I will haaavve some beef jerkeee if you perlease,' I said, trying not to laugh.

She looked me up and down like she couldn't quite work out where I was from. I suppose she might have thought I was a girl from South Carolina who had been living in Watford too long.

Beef jerky (a snack of smoked meat) and cheese were my foods of choice during the trip. On the Dr Atkins diet you could eat as much beef jerky as you liked because it's just pure protein, so Kenny and I stuffed our faces all the way through the journey. We arrived in San Francisco after seven hours on the road and stayed for two days exploring the sights of one of the world's most beautiful cities. I felt like I was taking a break from fame because there was no hassle and very little recognition.

After the stress and heartache of recent months, just being left alone to relax was a wonderful relief.

The break in LA was a chance to recharge my batteries and take stock. Pretty soon I'd realised that I couldn't do everything on my own any more and that managing my own career was just leaving me exhausted. I had talked to a few managers but I only wanted to work with someone I felt would do the job better than I could and who had better ideas. So, for a long time, I just muddled along. Then George's manager Andy Stephens offered to look after me. He had been around as a source of advice since I'd left the Spice Girls and I had always thought he was smart and charming but I had never wanted to tread on George's toes. When George said he was happy for me to go ahead, Andy seemed the natural choice.

The first thing Andy did was encourage me to start working on songs for my second album with Rick Nowells, one of the world's most successful songwriters. It was a daunting experience to go into the studio with someone new and with such a reputation. I had never met anyone who was even more pushy about getting things done in the studio than I was but Rick was really driven and worked me very hard. The working day would start at ten and continue until he was satisfied, even if that was one or two in the morning. His songwriting method was simple. He sat me down on a stool in his studio and just told me to sing. He would use the words and melodies I came up with to help me build a song. I was still very uncertain of my talents but Rick's writing style stretched me to my limits. He was a hard taskmaster but I will always be grateful to him and, as the work went on, we became great friends. It was very draining but the good news was that the second album was underway.

I returned home in May with George and Kenny by my side. They were coming with me to my mother's marriage to Steve. The wedding was being held in a sweet little country manor house in Rickmansworth, Hertfordshire. It was a beautiful sunny day, perfect for a wedding. Unfortunately, George, Kenny and I were already running late getting out of London and things went from bad to worse on the little country roads as we tried to navigate our way to the wedding. It was an unlikely picture as two pop stars from Watford and a Texan gentleman argued about which turning to take but eventually we made it.

As we pulled up I realised we had run into a familiar problem — the press. They were everywhere, all over the road in front of the venue and hanging from the trees trying to get the best picture. I felt so embarrassed and upset that I should have brought all this baggage and hassle down on an event like this. Fortunately, Mum was so happy and caught up in her special day that she didn't really seem to notice.

It was a strange situation to be attending my mum's romantic wedding and feeling proud of her. Wasn't this supposed to be the other way around? Weddings are always a bit of a test for single girls like me. I can't pretend I'd made marriage and romance a priority in my life because I was so focused on my career but Mum's wedding stirred those feelings. But I was so delighted for her and Steve that I put such thoughts aside and really enjoyed the day.

That spring I received my first award as a solo artist at the Capital Radio Awards in London. People say that awards don't mean anything and don't really matter but try telling that to somebody when they have actually won one! I won quite a few when I was in the Spice Girls but never on my own. I was nominated as Best Female along with Martine McCutcheon, my old friend Mel C and Gabrielle. It felt absolutely fantastic when they announced that I had won. As I told them in my speech, I was delighted and 'gobsmacked'.

George came to the ceremony with me that day, as he had the previous year. He was presenting an award. I had met the winner of the Best British Male Award that George was presenting, in passing, a couple of times before, but that afternoon was the first time I had really talked to Robbie Williams. It was the start of one of the best, most supportive and most speculated upon friendships of my life.

I was never a big fan of Take That. When I was living with the other Spice Girls in Maidenhead before we were signed to a record label, I was the odd one out. Being a little older than the other girls, I had idolised Wham! and Madonna but Rob's band had passed me by. I would try and join in with the other girls when they practised Take That's dance routines and sang along to all their lyrics but they could never mean as much to me. But I did think 'Back for Good' was a fantastic song.

Over the years, when I bumped into Rob, we got on fine but I didn't get to know him properly. The previous September he had performed in Watford and I had taken some friends to meet him backstage. Chris Briggs at EMI-Chrysalis was A&R man to both of us, so I knew we had that connection, but it was only after I left that night that I realised how many other experiences we shared. It struck me that Rob was the only person on earth who might be able to understand what happened to me with the Spice Girls because he experienced the same thing when he left Take That. We hadn't had a chance to talk for long that night but as I drove home, I remember thinking that I wanted to get to know him better.

Six months later I got my chance. Rob seemed to be winning everything that day at the Capital Radio Awards. The only award he didn't have a chance of winning was in the Best Female category because that was mine! After the show we got chatting and we were talking about the pressure fame had put on our lives and how difficult it was for others to understand how we felt. We really did have so much in common. That night he became Rob to me, not Robbie, because that's what his friends call him.

'Why don't you come up to my house?' I asked him. 'Just come and hang out at the weekend. It's completely private.'

Rob liked the idea and asked whether he could bring some friends. This wasn't a date we were planning but a fun weekend and I was happy for him to bring along as many people as he liked. The following Friday night, Rob, his best friend Jonny Wilkes, Jonny's girlfriend Nikki, another friend called Billy and my choreographer Luca came over to St Paul's for the first of many visits that summer. Right from the start it felt right. We were like a gang of overgrown children and Rob and I were the biggest kids of the lot.

Becoming famous can arrest your emotional development and sometimes it even sends it into reverse. Rob and I became famous in our late teens and early twenties respectively and from that point on, we lived in a world where everything was done for us. Most people start to take on more responsibility as they get older. They get a mortgage and start worrying about paying the bills but inside the bubble of fame, that doesn't happen. Somebody else usually takes care of the boring, adult side of life, leaving you all the time you want and all the money you need to play. The only problem comes when you are trying to find someone to play with. From that first weekend, Rob and I realised that in each other we had found the perfect playmate.

That first weekend the games were simple. St Paul's has an enormous garden and on the Saturday afternoon we had a marathon rounders session on the lawn. It might not sound very rock 'n' roll but that's because it wasn't. It was good, clean fun but it was such a rare experience for me. All my friends from Watford had their own lives and responsibilities. Rob and the others didn't have the same set of worries and it's hard to explain the thrill it gave me, to share the simple pleasures of a game of rounders with them in the evening sunshine. It was the first gang I'd been part of since the Spice Girls and it made me feel happy, as if I belonged.

The most popular games that summer were 'Mong' and 'Who's in the Bag?' (which we renamed 'Who's a dirty slag?'). Mong is probably the most stupid game on earth but we loved it. To play, you form a circle and throw a ball from one person to another at random. If you drop the ball you are given the letter 'M', do it again and you get the letter 'O' and on it goes until someone drops the ball a fourth time, spelling out the word M-O-N-G and losing the game. 'Who's in the Bag?' is a tiny bit more sophisticated but not much. We would divide ourselves into teams and then write the names of famous people on little pieces of paper which we would put into a bag. Team members would take it in turns to pull names out and try to give clues to their side about who they'd picked. The team that got the most right won. They were simple, childish games but they gave us hours and hours of fun, and if we ever got tired of them, St Paul's was perfect for hide and seek.

As the weekends became more regular, the games became more sophisticated and so did the toys. I have always been a speed freak and Rob's the same. That summer Rob and I made a new discovery, perfect for the rolling acres of St Paul's — monkey bikes.

Monkey bikes are like miniature motorbikes. They are fat and chunky and pretty powerful. At over £2000 each they are also the perfect toys for the young, rich and playful, and Rob and I bought three of them. The epic races took place on my lawn. The three competitors would usually be Rob, Jonny and me and the races would take place at top speed, day and night. There was an atmosphere of recklessness about that whole time. There was probably quite a lot at stake when you think about it — two pop stars at the top of their careers, whizzing around in the darkness at 30mph, narrowly missing trees and not too far from ploughing into each other. But, like kids, we weren't worried about the risks. I hadn't felt so free in a long time.

So Rob was my playmate. Everyone who saw us together at that time said the same thing: 'You're like brother and sister.' More than anything else, that's how I would describe it. I saw him as my male counterpart, like a long-lost twin brother. We had a shared sense of humour and an ability to know what the other was thinking about a person or situation. To other people, our connection seemed extraordinary but when I think how similar our lives have been, it makes sense.

Rob and I were both working-class teenage wannabes, dreaming of fame and fortune in our bedrooms and then, when we were barely adults, seeing those dreams come true beyond all our expectations. Neither of us found the reality of success and stardom easy to handle and in the end, we both took the same decision when the success got too big and the fame too overpowering — we walked away. Who else could really know how it felt to walk away from a massively successful group which you had helped to build, knowing it would carry on without you? Who else knew how it felt to make that decision in the media spotlight? And who else could understand all these things and also share my problems with addiction?

It felt so good to be able to talk to Rob and see my own experiences and responses reflected back. Nobody else could understand these things in quite the same way. St Paul's seemed a different place when he and the others were there — a place so full of life. I wasn't alone any more.

One Sunday, I took Rob and Luca to Cliveden, the stately home where I had celebrated 'Lift Me Up' reaching Number One with Chris Evans. Close to the famous pool they have a large hot tub, big enough for four or five people. It had been a great day, walking around the grounds and down to the lake, and this was the perfect way to end it. We were all sitting in the tub, Rob to my left and Luca to my right, when out of the corner of my eye I thought I saw Melanie Brown getting out of the pool and walking in our direction. I looked again, and, yes, it really was Mel.

'Oh my God,' I said, feeling suddenly nervous and excited.

'What?' said Rob.

'Over there, look, oh God, it's Mel.' I glanced over quickly. This was the first time I had seen her since that day two years earlier when I'd left the Spice Girls, and I didn't know what to expect if she saw me and came over.

'Call her over,' said Rob. 'Get it over with.'

He was right. I didn't want her to think I was ignoring her and the only thing that was holding me back was nerves. In the end, there was only one thing for it.

'Mel!' I called out. 'Do you want to join us?'

Mel looked up and clocked me, and just like me a few minutes earlier, she was a picture of shock and delight. Once she realised she wasn't seeing things, she let out one of her enormous laughs. For the next half an hour or so, it was just like old times. The sense of humour was still there and so too was our bond. It was quite a moment — two Spice Girls and Rob Williams chilling out in a hot tub where the Profumo Affair had happened! It was great to be able to spend some time with Mel again after two long years and it seemed to close that chapter of my life once and for all.

As the summer went on, the venue changed from St Paul's to Rob's house in west London. It was Euro 2000 and I found myself over at the house watching football with Rob and the others several times a week. Until now, we'd enjoyed a secret friendship but that had really only been possible because we'd spent most of our time together isolated out at St Paul's. By spending time at Rob's house in London, it was only a matter of time before our friendship became public property and the speculation that it was actually a romantic relationship would start.

We spent weeks dodging the paparazzi camped outside Rob's house before that night when Jonny smuggled me out in a rucksack and drove me away in Rob's Range Rover. Rob himself had gone ahead in my Aston Martin and we had met up on the road towards St Paul's before driving in convoy to my house for the night. There was a real sense of triumph in the air that evening. We had not only eluded the paparazzi for weeks but we had had a lot of fun doing it. We were playing a high-risk game of hide and seek and we were winning. But it wasn't to last.

The following week, as Euro 2000 drew to its conclusion (and even I was getting into it by now) we let our guard down. The evening had been spent with the usual group of people sitting in front of Rob's TV, watching the game and chatting. At about one o'clock in the morning, I was ready to drive home. We looked out of the window to see if there were photographers outside but the coast seemed to be clear so I decided to take my chance. Rob walked me to the door and out onto the street. At that moment, from inside a car, a flash bulb went off and they finally had their picture —

Robbie and Geri outside his home at 1 am. If you're a tabloid newspaper there was only one conclusion to be drawn.

It took a few days before *The Sun* ran the story. The headline? Robbie and Geri: It's Love. I suppose Robbie and Geri: They've Been Watching The Football might not have had the same ring to it or sold so many papers. They said that the picture showed me slipping away from Rob's home after a 'romantic evening together'. If your idea of a romantic evening with a guy is an evening in front of the telly with his mates before going home alone then fair enough, but it isn't mine!

One night that summer Rob suggested a new adventure for the gang.

'Why don't we all go on a massive holiday?' he said. 'We could hire a yacht and sail to the sunshine!'

I loved the idea but after chatting with Jonny and the others, quickly realised that a yacht might be a bit ambitious. Still, we could go somewhere, I thought, and set to work.

For most people, booking a holiday is a matter of popping into Thomas Cook or browsing through a few brochures before choosing a place you fancy. When you're famous, it's not that simple. Wherever you choose has to be hard to find and difficult to photograph. You have to know whether the place has high walls or nearby trees and you have to be careful how many people you tell about the location and what form of transport you use to get there. The best policy is always to book the place right at the last minute — that way you stand a better chance of avoiding the news leaking in time for the paparazzi to turn up and spoil the trip. Sometimes you can take all these precautions, as Rob and I did that August, and none of it works.

We had made a last-minute booking at a villa on the Côte d'Azur in the South of France in the mountains close to St Tropez. The villa was very secluded and the nearby beach resort was very small. We thought it would be the ideal place to get some sunshine and to hold an open house for family and friends for three weeks. There were a few of us going down there right from the beginning, including Jonny and Nikki, but we thought the best way to keep it all a secret was to travel separately. So we flew from London to Nice, meeting up at the airport before taking a helicopter to the villa. It was like a military operation and after the success of our rucksack escapade, we thought we had a chance of a little peace and quiet.

The villa was beautiful. It seemed to be the perfect place to hide. The pool area was very sheltered and was surrounded by palm trees and I immediately felt relaxed. Surely the press couldn't find us here? Rob and I had had a very busy and very successful year and we both needed a well-earned break. We decided to hire a moped so that we could go for drives up on the mountain roads that surrounded the villa. Rob drove while I hung on for dear life on the back. Back at the villa with the gang, we'd sunbathe and play backgammon or one of our silly games. I felt totally at ease. The summer of 2000 was getting better and better.

A few days into the trip, a call came from Andy Stephens.

'Have you seen the papers, Geri?' he said.

'No,' I said. 'What's in them? Has something happened?'
'I'll fax them through.'

A few minutes later the fax whirred into action and a blurred black and white copy of that morning's *Sun* came through. A picture of me and Rob on our moped dominated the page below the headline I LOVE MY THROBBIE. Alongside were three more photographs showing the two of us sunbathing by the pool and floating on lilos. The story underneath gave sketchy details of our 'love' and presented the holiday as a romantic break for two in a love nest in the South of France.

No matter how many times you find yourself staring out from the pages of the newspaper, caught in a private moment by a photographer who must have been hiding far away in the bushes or perched precariously in a tree, you never really get used to it. You feel like somebody has taken something from you, creeping in uninvited to steal your private moments away for public consumption. My sense of peace and relaxation had been based on a naïve belief that we had escaped that sort of attention. In reality, the paparazzi had been there all along watching our every move.

I took the fax out to Rob and the others by the pool and showed them the story. We all knew how determined the paparazzi were but we couldn't understand how they had found us so quickly after all the precautions we had taken. We decided there must have been a leak of some kind but couldn't work out where from. Drivers? Travel agents? Someone at the airport? In the end, it didn't matter who it was. It only ever takes one person to leak information like that and at the end of the day, if someone is going to betray you, it's impossible to prevent it.

We sat by the pool for a while that afternoon, speculating on the source of the information. Suddenly, our lovely holiday was at risk of being overtaken by this invading force and we could react in one of two ways — we could spend the rest of our time hiding from the press, holed up inside our villa, or we could carry on regardless. Rob made the decision for us.

'I don't know about you, but I'm not going to let this spoil my holiday.'

'Absolutely,' I said. 'It's nothing new after all.'

We decided that we would spend the next day down at the beach even though we knew there could be press around. There were to be many more pictures of that holiday and many more inaccurate stories about our so-called celebrity romance.

The funny thing about the *Sun* article that day was that despite their story, the pictures seemed to disprove what they were saying. If me and Rob were really 'so in love' like the story said, then they must have been very disappointed with the photographs they got. They didn't provide a scrap of evidence. I had to laugh at the part of the story that mentioned me 'wrapping my arms around his chest as we went for a spin on his scooter'. Wouldn't you? On a mountain road with no crash helmet? That wasn't about love so much as wanting to avoid falling to a certain death down a French mountainside!

The numbers of guests at the villa grew as the weeks passed. My old friend Janine from Watford came to stay for a while and so did my sister Natalie. George's house was just down the road so he and Kenny visited and Rob's songwriting partner Guy Chambers brought along his wife and baby. Despite the problems with the paparazzi, we all had a fantastic time. It really was one of the best holidays of my life.

The friendship and support Rob and his friends offered to me that summer had allowed me to really enjoy a break from work for the first time in years. They also protected me from the worst excesses of my eating disorder. I was less likely to react against the Atkins diet or use food like a drug when I was with good friends. It's obvious, really, but the risks of a binge were that much greater when I was alone or unhappy. Rob understands the way addiction works because he has his own struggles and I think the whole gang helped us both stay on course.

On our holiday in the South of France I ate better than I had in a long time. We had our own cook who prepared lovely fresh food and we all ate together out by the pool or around the kitchen table. Back home, rather than try to deny myself all week long, I would follow the Dr Atkins diet from Monday to Saturday and take Sunday off. I called it 'Sod it Sunday' because I could eat what I wanted. Cakes were a favourite. I thought this was a way of controlling the problem without having to really struggle and I could always work extra hard in the gym on Monday morning.

In July, Jerry Hall had told me about her trainer, a Norwegian guy called Torje, who had helped her shape up for her naked performance in *The Graduate* in the West End. I thought Jerry looked svelte and gorgeous so I was very interested in giving him a try. Before meeting Torje I had always trained to excess. I would work really hard on a bike or treadmill for 30 minutes and hope to burn off as much fat as I could and sweat as much as possible. It was painfully hard work but I thought it was the only way. Torje had different ideas. He told me to strap a heart monitor onto my chest and work out more slowly but for a longer period, keeping my heart rate at between 115 and 130 bpm. That way, he said, I would burn off the fat more rapidly. At first I didn't trust him because it felt too easy, like going for a fast walk, but I kept going. He obviously really knew his stuff, though, and it wasn't long before I started seeing the benefits and losing weight.

I was starting to really work on my yoga, which was helping too. Probably the most famous picture of the holiday in the South of France was taken on the beach when I was doing my yoga while Rob and the others sunbathed. After that, two things happened — everyone asked me about yoga and I started to hear compliments about my figure. Something was changing and it felt great. Of course, I was still clearly obsessed with weight loss. I didn't realise it at the time but I was still only one serious binge away from going into complete reverse.

I had tried to hide the seriousness of my obsession with diet and body image from the gang of friends but I couldn't hide it from Rob. He recognised that my relationship with food was addictive. But I wasn't ready to hear the solution he was suggesting.

'Have you thought about getting some help with it?' he asked.

'Why?' I said. 'It's all right, Rob, it's under control.'

And at that time it seemed to me it was. I was getting thinner and bingeing less. This time, I thought, I might just have cracked it.

Going home in the autumn was difficult. I hate the end of summer but this time I felt my spirits start to dip almost as soon as I got back to Britain. Something happens to me as the nights get darker and the sun disappears; I can feel an emotional heaviness descend. My father died at that time of year and the wind and rain of October and November in England always reminds me of his death. And sure enough, it wasn't long before I could feel myself sinking.

I knew I didn't want to spend any more cold months rattling around at home in St Paul's. I had enjoyed spending time with Rob and his friends and I didn't want to isolate myself in the middle of nowhere again. Inside I think I knew how fragile I was. I decided to rent a tiny flat above a restaurant called Julie's in Portland Road, Notting Hill. I thought I might spend two or three nights a week there, but it wasn't long before I found myself there full time. I had enjoyed some wonderful times at St Paul's but emotionally, I was starting to detach myself from it. It was a trophy house more than a home and I had learned enough to know it wasn't the right place for me to be any more.

One way to ease the seasonal blues was a trip to LA. I thought I'd get some more songwriting done with Rick Nowels and I hoped that a trip to George and Kenny's LA home would make me feel better. The album had been progressing since I had started working with Rick in the spring and I had worked with lots of different writers and producers, including my old friends at Absolute and Annie Lennox's producer Steve Lipson and the songwriter Peter Vettese. Rob had also been giving me a musical education. Believe it or not, I had never really listened to the Beatles' music until that summer because it wasn't played in our house when I was growing up. So he turned me onto them and Led Zeppelin, who were never heard in our house either. It was amazing to discover this new musical world and I wanted to get that influence across in the work I did with Rick.

Whenever I drove from George and Kenny's house in Beverly Hills to Rick's studio, I would find myself stuck in a traffic jam on Sunset Boulevard. The advertising hoardings that tower over Sunset are designed to catch the eye but as I crawled along the street one morning I was lucky not to lose my concentration and bang into the car ahead. In front of me, rising ten storeys into the sky and dressed from head to toe in leather, were my old friends Mel, Mel, Victoria and Emma. The Spice Girls were back and judging by the new look, they were finally giving r'n'b a shot. It was strange to drive down the road every morning on my way to work and find them staring down at me but once I got used to it, it became a daily ritual. 'Morning, girls!' I'd say as they came into view. 'How are you today?'

Since I had left the group they had actually recorded very little new material, spending most of their time concentrating on their solo careers. But now they were back with the r'n'b album I had always suspected they wanted to make. I had mixed feelings about the comeback. Part of me hoped that the Spice Girls brand was strong enough to survive wherever they went musically but I also knew that this was the first time the band had really put something together without my input.

In the end, the new music was so different from the group I had been in that most of those feelings seemed irrelevant. The girls had worked with some of the hottest producers in America to come up with a very authentic r'n'b sound. As usual, the Spice Girls went into the charts at Number One with the first single, 'Holler', but otherwise things had certainly changed. Who can say what would have happened if I'd stayed? There's a good chance I would have ended up on that enormous billboard looking *very* uncomfortable trying to convince the world that Geri from Watford was really an r'n'b diva! Perhaps it was better that it worked out the way it did.

Work continued on my new album into November and was going well. I was staying at George and Kenny's and spent a lot of time hanging out with Kenny between studio sessions with Rick. There were a few other people around in LA at the time who I knew through Kenny — some basketball players and a few others. I would sometimes go for a drink with them in Hollywood but none of them were close friends. So, when Kenny had to go on a business trip I found myself alone again.

For a long time I had looked to external things to explain my feelings of unhappiness and low self-esteem. I must be unhappy because I need a boyfriend or maybe because I'm still too fat. Perhaps I should change my hair colour or buy that new dress. When I was in the Spice Girls I blamed Ginger for my problems. I would tell myself that I could deal with my demons if I could escape from the cartoon character that had taken over my life. However, as I sat in George and Kenny's LA home one evening at the end of 2000, Ginger was long gone but the feelings were still there. I was alone with Geri and I was running out of excuses. It had been one of the best years of my life — my solo career had really taken off and I had made some fantastic friends — but the minute I was alone the demons were back as strong as ever.

Hello low self-esteem!

Welcome back, fear!

Come on in, anxiety!

I didn't think that the reasons for my feelings were actually internal ones, even though when I was alone, with only myself for company, the intensity of those feelings became unbearable. And when that happened I would use sugar as a drug to deal with them. To all intents and purposes I was a sugar addict and, once again, I was slipping out of control.

It was a relief when Kenny arrived home from his business trip but it didn't last long. He was planning to go to Europe to see George, so I was going to have to get through Thanksgiving by myself. Rather than spend the holiday alone, I decided to tackle the problem head on and invite a few of the basketball crowd and others on the social scene to come over for dinner. I was going to play the hostess.

America has the best take-away food in the world. My favourite was a service called 'Can't Cook, Won't Cook'. It offers food from twenty different restaurants and every style of food you could possibly want, all via one easy-to-dial phone number. I am not the world's best cook but I am pretty good at ordering in! I ordered turkey with all the trimmings, roast potatoes, mashed potatoes, sweetcorn, pumpkin pie and as many sticky, rich and chocolatey puddings and cakes as I could find.

When we sat down for dinner, I had the smallest plate, limiting myself to a little bit of turkey, some vegetables and not much else. Potatoes weren't allowed and pudding was out of the question. I denied myself as everyone else tucked into the food but even then they barely scratched the surface of what I had bought. After dinner we sat down and watched *Pulp Fiction* on video. It was a nice evening, and at about eleven o'clock people started preparing to leave. While they did, I busied myself cleaning up after dinner. I stacked all the dishes in the dishwasher and cleaned up the kitchen and then turned to the piles of untouched food, mostly puddings, that were on the counter. I knew the dangers of having that sort of food in the house so I decided to throw all the leftovers — cakes, puddings, turkey and potatoes — into a bin liner which I tied and took outside to the garage. I wasn't looking forward to being on my own but I was determined to stop myself from bingeing.

By midnight everyone had gone and I was alone. I decided that the safest thing to do was sleep so I undressed, put on a T-shirt and got ready for bed. Then a little voice inside my head said, 'Come on, Geri, why don't you have some cake? There's plenty outside in the garage. I'm sure you can rescue it.' The idea was so disgusting but the voice, like a devil on my shoulder, got louder and louder and more and more insistent. So then, in some sort of trance-like state, I found myself opening the back door and walking to the pile of rubbish bags in the corner. I spotted the one I had taken out half an hour before and knelt down, my knees cold against the rough garage floor, and untied it.

Inside, the cakes and puddings were crushed out of shape and mixed in with the half-eaten Thanksgiving dinner but that didn't seem to matter any more. It was too late. I needed my sugar fix.

I reached inside the bin bag, fished out some chocolate cake and stuck it in my mouth, savouring the flavour. Inside, I felt a terrible sense of shame and self-disgust as I knelt there but I couldn't stop myself. I ate and ate and ate and ate until I was so full, all I could do was sleep.

In the next few days, binge followed binge followed binge. I drew the curtains, stopped answering the phone and just ordered more and more food from the take-out service. I would tell myself that I'd start my diet tomorrow and used that promise to myself to justify over-ordering and pretty much cleaning George and Kenny's kitchen out at the same time. This went on for three days straight until, finally, I got down on my knees and, crying my eyes out, begged for a way out.

'Oh God, if you are there, please help me.'

There was no bolt of lightning or heavenly reply but instead, there was a moment of real clarity. At last I realised that I couldn't control this monster any more. I needed to go and find help, fast.

It was the decision that saved my life.

Love is the Only Light

It was only a few miles from George's house in Beverly Hills to suburban Santa Monica but the drive that day was one of the most difficult journeys of my life. As I made my way through the LA traffic my heart was beating fast and I had butterflies in my stomach. I knew the dread of walking out in front of 100,000 people. I had even sung 'Happy Birthday', unaccompanied, to the Prince of Wales, but nothing had prepared me for the anxiety of this moment.

As I parked my car outside the plain-looking community hall and climbed out into the winter sunshine, I just wanted to run away. My mind raced with reasons not to walk across the small courtyard and go inside the building. How can I, Geri Halliwell, put myself through this? What if someone recognises me? Can't I just go home and come back another day? But then, slowly and reluctantly, I forced myself to put one foot in front of the other and walk towards the entrance. Deep inside, I knew that I really had no choice any more.

On that night a few days after Thanksgiving, I had finally realised that I had to do something or the situation would spiral out of control. I believed that my addiction would kill me if I didn't take it on. I didn't know how long it would take to get me but I knew that in the end, it would. If I continued consuming so much sugar I could develop diabetes, or the trauma of vomiting might one day trigger a heart attack. The most serious risk, though, was depression. I didn't know how long I would be able to go on living like this. Carrying on as I was seemed intolerable — why would I want to live if I couldn't change?

So later that same night, my belly painfully full, I had logged onto the internet at George's house and typed in the words 'eating disorders'. The first result, right at the top of the page, gave the name of a therapist in LA specialising in the problem. Her name and number on the screen made it all feel very real. Was I really ready to seek help and to admit my problem? Was I really ready to label myself? In the end, an instinct stronger than pride forced me to the phone. I called the number and left a message on her machine asking if I could go and see her. There was no turning back now.

After my first appointment with the therapist, I had thought of Rob's words in the summer when he'd suggested I get some help. His experience told him I had a serious problem and, though he hadn't seen me overeating or caught me making myself sick, he knew my relationship with food was very unhealthy.

When I described my behaviour to the therapist at our first meeting a day or so later, she suggested that I would benefit from group therapy. The thought of attending meetings with complete strangers and talking about my problems was incredibly daunting. In the end, though, I had to think about the rock bottom I had hit when I got down on my knees that night. I had to decide whether I was brave enough to save myself from that fate. I realised I was in a desperate situation and I had to overcome my fears and get the help I so badly needed. So I took the number of the hotline and called. The following day, 7th December 2000, I got in my car and drove to Santa Monica.

Having arrived at the meeting I still had to overcome my self consciousness and to some extent my vanity, to persuade myself to go inside. This was not a very glamorous, Geri Halliwell thing to be doing. As I looked tentatively around the room, I was struck by the variety of different types in the group of what must have been thirty to forty people. They came in all shapes and sizes. Some were overweight, others thin and some seemed 'normal' sized. Most were women although there were more men than I had expected and I could tell that they came from all walks of life — young mothers, businessmen, factory workers and students — the whole spectrum. That first meeting gave me a chance to reconnect with the lives of real people after so many years in the celebrity bubble. Here, everyone was equal and fame and fortune counted for nothing.

As I sat there listening to their stories, all of which in some way, echoed my own experiences, my tension started to ease and I had an overwhelming feeling that I had come to the right place. Just the knowledge that everyone at that first meeting shared the same types of insanity, self obsession, sense of isolation, self loathing — gave me strength. I was not alone after all.

Attending a support group for the first time is difficult enough for anybody but my fame added an extra layer of worry. My first concern had been that somebody in the group would recognise me and say something or go to the press. In reality, I needn't have worried. The American public remembered Ginger Spice but they hadn't really caught on to Geri Halliwell. It wasn't at all surprising that nobody made a connection between the timid figure sitting silently in the corner and Ginger Spice. In any case, any kind of support group depends on anonymity and all genuine members believe strongly in the importance of keeping details of the others in the group private. I was among friends.

Getting help was a big step for me. I was confessing a truth that I had only just accepted myself — that I had an eating disorder and I needed help to control it. Over the years I had been caught in a cycle of starvation diets and dangerous overeating. Now I was an addict. Food was my drug and I would use it as a reward, a punishment and a way to escape my feelings.

I knew I was going to have to work hard to control my problem. Even though I would have loved for someone to wave a magic wand and make me OK again I knew that was impossible. Although I had denied my problem for so long, I knew that its roots were very deep and to understand it and beat it would mean a lot of painful work on myself. This wasn't a quick fix.

The key to recovery, I soon learned, was abstinence. What that means depends on the individual — it will mean something different to an anorexic person than it will to someone who overeats. For me it means not bingeing. I have binged for many reasons — boredom, excitement, loneliness, stress — and my binges are very closely linked to those periods during which I deny myself food or strictly control what I eat. My goal would be to avoid those binges. To succeed I would have to address all of the factors that made them happen.

As part of this process I had started writing a diary again. I had recorded my thoughts and feelings on and off since I was a teenager but lately had let the habit slip. Now, I was finding that it was a useful way of understanding my feelings and coming clean about my condition:

Thurs 7th Dec 2000.
My name is Geri I am recovering
compulsive overeater bulimic anorexic

Admitting such things in a diary is one thing, though. Admitting that I was a 'compulsive overeater, anorexic, bulimic' to the other people in the group was much harder but forcing myself to do so changed my life. People often talk about a weight being lifted from their shoulders and that was exactly how it felt — like a physical sensation. Confessing my problem seemed to reduce my compulsion to binge and take away some of its power. I immediately felt stronger but I realised that this was just the beginning of the road to recovery.

Although I knew I could completely rely on the others in the group to respect my anonymity, I was less lucky with my old friends, the British press. Most people who seek help for their addictions can choose whether they tell anybody else about it. For me, the option just wasn't there — sooner or later the press would get hold of the story. It didn't take them long.

One day, as I left a group therapy meeting and walked to my car, I found myself surrounded by a scrum of paparazzi and tabloid reporters. It can't have been too difficult to find me — I was followed by the paparazzi in LA from time to time anyway — but it still came as a terrible shock when they pounced. It was so distressing to think the story would be all over the British papers within hours. My mind was racing. *I better call Mum, I should let Andy know.* As well as feeling furious with the press for my own sake, I also felt guilty for attracting the media circus to such a private place. What had the other group members done to deserve this attention? As I battled my way through the crowd and into my car I saw a familiar face out of the corner of my eye. It was a young woman I had seen in the group a few days before. She seemed to want to talk to me.

'Geri,' she said, 'just how serious is your eating problem?'

She had a microphone. She was from the press and she had been spying on me all along. Even now I find it hard to believe how low some people will stoop for a story.

After that, I changed my routine. I got a list of all the meetings in the Los Angeles area and varied where I attended and how regularly. The only good aspect of the story getting out was that now they had their scoop there was less chance of them trying to catch me speaking at a meeting again. After headlines in Britain like GINGER THE BINGER there wasn't much privacy left to protect.

It had been so hard to find the courage to seek help but I was feeling the benefits already. My true strength was about to be put to the test. My recording work in LA was done for the time being and it was time to go home, just in time for Christmas when bingeing becomes a national pastime.

The first thing I needed to do to recover was learn to eat sensibly — no more starvation diets and no more binges. Usually the more stable eating habits of my friends and family were a good influence but at Christmas the opposite is true — everybody 'normal' is stuffing their face. For me, walking into that world of mince pies and double cream, Christmas cake and figgy puddings was like sending a recovering alcoholic for a week's holiday to the Munich Beer Festival. Attempting it might be brave but it would also be foolish. So, when I got back to my London flat, I called my mum to let her know that I wouldn't be home for Christmas this year.

'Oh that's a shame, Geri,' she said. I could tell from her voice that she was really disappointed. Christmas itself wasn't all that important to her but it did give us a chance to see each other for an extended period. I had hardly been in the UK since I'd left to go on holiday with Rob so I understood how she felt. 'I'm sorry,' I said, 'but I love you 365 days of the year, not just on this one. So do you mind if I just opt out this year?'

Luckily Mum was very understanding but now I had to decide what to do instead. I had spent the last few weeks examining my own feelings and facing up to my problem. Self-analysis was an important part of my struggle for abstinence but it was also exhausting. By Christmas I wanted a break from myself. As a solution, I tried to look for ways to think about other people instead.

A few weeks before Christmas I had received a letter from the Make A Wish Foundation — a charity that tries to fulfil the dreams of sick and dying children — about a sixteen-year-old girl called Debbie Curran who had been a big fan of mine since my time in the Spice Girls. She had asked to meet me. The letter said that Debbie, who had suffered from cystic fibrosis since she was a baby, was at the Royal Brompton Hospital in London waiting for a heart and lung transplant. Unless she got the transplant she would soon die but there was no guarantee she would get one or that she would survive the operation if she did.

I try to do what I can for charity and have visited many seriously ill fans over the years. It has become a cliché but it is still true that the courage and bravery of these kids is an inspiration. They seem to be able to accept the unfairness of their illnesses without complaining and are more concerned about the feelings of their loved ones than their own pain. Fame seems pretty unimportant when compared to that sort of bravery. I got in touch with Make A Wish and asked them to fix a date for me to see Debbie.

I arrived at the Royal Brompton Hospital one evening not long before Christmas and was shown up to the ward where Debbie was in a special room. Her mum Philomena was waiting outside. She told me how much of a fan Debbie was and how thrilled she was about meeting me. Before I went in to see her, I had a quick glance through the window in the door. There, lying on the bed, connected by tubes to a machine, was a beautiful young girl. She was sixteen but looked more like a twelve- or thirteen-year-old and she reminded me of Audrey Hepburn — the same beautiful dark eyes and dark hair.

As I walked in the door I could see the evidence that she was a fan of mine all over the walls. There were pictures from my days in the Spice Girls as well as every phase of my solo career. But those weren't the pictures that caught my attention. It was obvious that there was a rival Ginger for

Debbie's affections — Chris Evans. His picture was everywhere too and there were even pictures of him with Debbie that had obviously been taken right there in her hospital room. As I sat down on the bed and we started to chat, Debbie explained that she had asked to meet him too and that he had been in several times.

It was surprising that Chris and I didn't bump into each other going back and forth from Debbie's room. I hadn't seen him since the end of our brief relationship and now visiting Debbie had brought it all back to me. It was a strange coincidence and part of me felt as if I was competing for the affections of this little girl knowing I wasn't the only star in her life. I quickly reminded myself that such unpleasant feelings were completely trivial compared with what Debbie was going through.

Debbie was a genuinely extraordinary, clever, funny girl and she was great company. I would find myself popping into the hospital unannounced, just to spend time watching crappy TV programmes with her. I remember going over on Saturday nights to lie down next to her and watch the National Lottery show. She had an extra special quality that drew me (and Chris) back to see her again and again and I was deeply affected by meeting her. Just before Christmas I wrote in my diary:

> Saturday 23rd December 2000.
>
> The blessing I have received is to meet such an angel as Debbie. She is amazing. I am actually so in awe of her. Her strength and courage. Her radiance. I pray for her heart and lungs to be donated, let her live.

On Christmas Day itself, I went to a youth centre in Brixton run by the charity Kids Company which was providing somewhere for children with difficult backgrounds to enjoy the day, have a roast dinner and have some fun. The kids seemed pleased to see me and I remember some of the toughest little nuts in the group acting all hard but then, when I was leaving, asking me for hugs and Christmas kisses. It was such a relief to avoid the excesses of the Christmas season and do a little bit of good at the same time. I had made the right decision and I was still abstinent. I had avoided bingeing.

New Year was going to be a real treat. I was spending the rest of the holiday skiing in the Swiss resort of Gstaad with Rob, Jonny, Nikki and some of the others. Since our summer holiday, Rob and I had both been working hard on our records but he had always been there for me when I needed him. When I hit my lowest point with my eating disorder in November, Rob and I would speak on the phone every day. It didn't matter how busy he was at the time, he was always available to share his knowledge and understanding of the pressures — fame and addiction. He was very, very supportive and I will never forget what he did for me.

The trip to Gstaad was just what I needed, a relaxing break with friends. I was also very excited about the skiing. I had been to Ralph Lauren and bought a fantastic black leather ski outfit with a built-in thermostat to keep me warm on the slopes! It was the sort of thing a Bond Girl would wear and I thought I looked the bee's knees. I was like Toad of Toad Hall with all the garb. Unfortunately, any positive impression given by my appearance was blown as soon as I got onto the slopes.

The last time I'd skied was pre-Spice Girls and I was a natural. I just strapped on my skis and off I went. Not this time. I had no idea what to do and had lost all that youthful bravado. One morning I was trying to get onto the T-bar lift to take me to the top of the slope but I was finding it a bit tricky. I ended up half on and half off, being dragged up the slope like a complete nerd wearing the coolest ski-suit you have ever seen. In the end I had to call for Rob to get me down.

After that I decided skiing wasn't for me and anyway it was *so* yesterday. I would try snowboarding. I went to the ski store and bought myself a state-of-the-art snowboarding outfit and went back to the mountain. I was fine when it came to setting off down the slope but I couldn't get the turning motion right to allow me to stop. The only way I could work out to stop myself from flying down the mountain to a certain death was throwing myself onto my bum. The result was a bruise the size of a grapefruit. After that I stuck to ice skating and long walks.

On New Year's Eve we went to a party at the hotel where we were staying. Unfortunately it turned out to be a banquet more than a party and I found it very uncomfortable to be so close to temptation. It was exactly what I had tried to avoid at Christmas and Rob could see I was getting agitated.

'You want to get out of here?' he said.

'Do you mind?' I asked, grateful for his understanding.

So we all left and went to hang out in one of the rooms and play cards. When midnight came we went outside into the freezing black night to watch the fireworks bring in the New Year.

Tuesday   2nd Jan 2001.
26th days Abstinence. Now it feels like a lifeline
In the last 26 days I have endured the press
/ physical withdrawal 4 sugar, panic, loneliness,
Insecurities Christmas, two parties New Year
, a holiday, travel feeling lost.
And I didnt binge! I can survive.
I can endure these feelings good and bad.
Its been a million times better than
where I was 26 days ago.

A couple of weeks or so into the New Year I got a call from Philomena, Debbie's mum, to let me know that a heart and lung donor had been found for Debbie. She'd had the operation but it was too early to tell whether it had been a success. Debbie was in intensive care fighting for her life. I was desperate to see her and Philomena wanted me to go in, hoping I might be able to get through to her daughter and help her to recover.

When I arrived, Philomena and other family members were gathered around Debbie's bed. She was unconscious and only breathing with the help of a machine. Philomena pulled back the covers to show me the scars on Debbie's body. I had never seen anything like it in my life and I just felt so helpless. I could tell that she was only just holding onto life. Philomena wanted me to play Debbie 'Love Is The Only Light', a song I had written for her and recently recorded. Although it seemed pointless, I put it on and at one point I felt her stir a little and lightly squeeze my hand. I clung onto that tiny squeeze as a sign of hope.

A few days later I was working out at home before going to the studio when my mobile rang. It was Philomena.

'It's Debbie,' she said. 'She's gone. She passed away last night.'

Philomena sounded broken and exhausted. She had just said goodbye to her beautiful, exceptional daughter. What could I say to do justice to the way she felt? I did my best to comfort her and then, as she rang off, collapsed onto the floor in tears, screaming at God and asking him why he would let such a thing happen. Life seemed so cruel and unfair and I felt waves of anger and grief at the loss.

Then I remembered Debbie's serenity and calmness. She'd never complained. She had always said she'd rather risk the operation than stay as she was. At least this way she'd tried.

Sunday 28th January 2007

I found out that Debbie died. She was inspiring. The courage, the perseverance. I was amazed at the strength of this beautiful, delicate child. But she died. Why? Where is the justification? I can only imagine that Debbie was too good for this world. I know the greatest gift I can give to Debbie is to to take what she taught me into my own life, embrace my life and appreciate every passing breath that I take for granted. I am blessed to have met such a girl. Thank you Debbie for choosing me. You wished for a star but instead I met an angel. Thank you.

It would take a whole book on its own to really explain the recovery process I have been through. All I can do is try to convey how profoundly it affected my life from the moment I got help in December 2000. I can honestly say it has been the most painful thing I have ever done, and the most rewarding.

I didn't know it at the time but the moment I picked up the phone and asked for help, I took my first step on the road to recovery. That simple step marked the end of years and years of denial because I was confessing that I was powerless over food and that my life was out of control as a result.

I began to realise how dishonest I had been to myself and to my friends and family for so long. I was living a double life, giving the impression that everything was fine and that my eating problems were over when I knew that I had been controlling and bingeing. Now I just wanted to be honest.

The first person I had to be honest with was myself. I had accepted I was powerless over food but now I had to look for the reasons. And when I did, I realised that my addiction was not the disease, but the symptom. Insane as it sounds, I even found a reason to be grateful for my problem.

Tuesday 2nd January 2001.
I have to thank my eating disorder because it gave
me a coping mechanism to manage the life
I couldn't cope with. Who knows where I would
have been without it? I must thank what I used
but now it's time to say goodbye. I shall remember
all the times you have been there for me when I
couldn't cope, when the pain was too much for me
to endure. When I was alone you were my friend,
when I had no-one I felt I could turn to, you
helped me love myself. You saved me from
suicide.

The truth is that my eating disorder was my way of coping with life. When life got too much, I used food as my crutch. When I felt unable to cope with real-life situations, I used food as a way to avoid the issue. Without it I might have gone crazy, I might have killed myself. For years it had served its purpose but now it was out of control.

The time had come to tackle the underlying problems that I used food to run away from. Why couldn't I cope? What exactly was the problem? I had so much to be grateful for in my life. I had enjoyed huge success and reaped enormous financial rewards. I had travelled the world and experienced extraordinary things but I had still found myself down on my knees eating chocolate cake from a dustbin because that felt better than being alone with myself. How could this be? I could only explain by looking at my past.

I came from a poor family and a broken home and had always felt like I was the odd one out, the token working-class girl in Watford Grammar School. But these things alone can't really explain my eating disorder. They do help to explain why I was so hungry for fame from an early age — after all, they are the classic conditions needed to produce a wannabe. I think the real explanation has its roots in the death of my father in November 1993 and the fact that six months later — still reeling from my loss — I walked into a London rehearsal studio and auditioned for the group that would become the Spice Girls.

In the weeks after Dad died I wandered around in a daze. I felt robbed, angry and deprived — I had lost my father and I could never have him back. All I could focus on was my desperate desire for fame and losing Dad had given it a fresh impetus. Now I wanted to succeed in honour of his memory and it felt as if time was running out for me as it had for him. As a result, I put myself through audition after audition and was rejected every time. I wondered what was wrong with me and time and time again I told myself the problem was my body, my weight. If I wanted to make it, I would have to be thinner and that meant cutting back dangerously on what I ate. Here in a time of emotional turmoil was something I could control. Six months after Dad's death I was living on a diet of apples, crushed ice and coffee — I was a dangerously skinny anorexic.

On the day before I went to the Spice Girls audition, I described the depths of my despair in my diary:

It is crippling me, I cannot move, It paralyses my rational thought. I enjoy nothing. I am existing in a lonely world of turmoil and confusion. I can count on one hand how many times I've laughed this year.

It would be easier if I had no will left. I could join my daddy. No I can't be a bloody quitter.

The next morning I woke at dawn and made myself get up and go to the audition that changed my life. I didn't realise it then but I had taken an invisible fork in the road which — for better *and* for worse — directed me towards fame.

What would have happened if I had stayed in bed that morning? Maybe, eventually, tired of rejection, I would have given up on my dreams of fame and fortune and settled down in Watford. Away from the pressures and stresses of fame I might have found help for my illness and counselling for my grief much more quickly. In the end, I can never know. Did fame save me from even deeper despair or just prolong my agony?

Over the New Year of 1994/95 all alone in the house I shared with the girls in Maidenhead, I had binged to frightening excess until, desperate, I had gone to Watford General Hospital and checked into the Psychiatric Unit. Ten days numbed on Prozac seemed to straighten me out and I was able to return to the world of Spice but I remember feeling disappointed that no one had tried to understand the reasons for my problems — they'd just patched me up with drugs and a diet sheet and let me go. I was none the wiser. Eighteen months later the Spice Girls were Number One all over the world and for a long time fame and success allowed me to run away from the pain that had taken me to that psychiatric ward in the first place.

I had a new purpose in life and in Ginger, a new personality to hide behind. But running away was exhausting and when the feelings caught up with me as they inevitably did from time to time, I used food to escape. In the end, on my knees in LA, I knew I had to stop running and face up to my problem.

Abstinence felt great but at the same time it was hard work. Like taking off a pair of dark sunglasses on a sunny day, I could see everything much more clearly but the brightness hurt my eyes. In the first few weeks after I had found help, I was caught up in the excitement of my new challenge but, as time went on, it became more and more difficult to deal with my feelings and the continual effort of abstinence and the temptation grew stronger.

Thursday 1st February 2007 (56 days abstinence)

No matter what. That's a great saying for me

No matter what don't overeat, no matter what protect my abstinence, no matter what don't forget I have a disease. I am compulsive overeater, spiritually sick. I need high-maintenance like a child.

Oh my God. Only by the skin of my teeth did I remain abstinent today.

As I struggled to stop myself giving in to my craving, I was preparing for a new cycle of work. By February I had put the finishing touches to my second album which I had called *Scream If You Wanna Go Faster*, being the title of a song I had written on the day of my first recovery meeting. It was about all the things I did to avoid staying still and dealing with my feelings. It was also by far the most rock and roll sounding song I had ever recorded, inspired by Rob playing me Led Zeppelin during the summer.

The shoot for the album cover in Miami was long and stressful and, as usual, I was fighting with feelings of inadequacy in front of a camera. Successfully stopping my bingeing had made me lose weight but that didn't completely silence the voices that told me I was still too fat and I couldn't escape the stresses of my job. I had always found travel difficult and exhausting and on the plane back from Miami to London after the shoot, the pressure of remaining abstinent began to tell. I decided the best thing to do was to take a sleeping tablet and crash out for the whole flight. As it turned out the pill didn't just knock me out, it also weakened my resolve.

I slept through most of the flight but woke up as the plane descended into London feeling groggy and disorientated. When I feel the urge to binge it's as if there are two voices whispering in my ear.

'Don't do it,' says the abstinent voice. 'You've got to stay strong. Wait till you get home and have a proper breakfast.'

'Once can't hurt,' argued the voice of my craving. 'You're tired. You need some extra fuel. Don't be so hard on yourself.'

The debate raged on inside my head as I made my way through the arrivals hall and out towards where the taxis were waiting. The abstinent voice was telling me that I was nearly clear now, just a few feet away from the safety of a ride home. But the voice of my craving had other ideas.

'Sweet shop!' it said to me. 'Come on, Geri, you could do with some energy after that long flight. Just have a look.'

So, like a zombie after the flight and the pill, I allowed myself to walk into the shop. Once I had crossed that line there was no way back. The craving voice had convinced me. Surely a few sweets couldn't do any harm? I spent the journey home bingeing on the chocolate and sweets I had been working so hard to resist for so long. When I got home, I went out and bought some more.

> Wednesday 21st Feb 2001.
> Well yesterday I broke my abstinence. I was gutted. After all I've been it finally came. I couldn't help myself. I couldn't understand it. I've done the footwork but it looks like I have lessons to learn. I was on a sleeping tablet which tells me I can't take mood altering drugs. To be honest I've got to stop seeing my abstinence as a goal and just as a day of freedom – a daily reprieve.

Initially, the sense of failure and hopelessness I felt was overpowering. After all this time and all of the temptations and stresses, I had weakened. If any part of me believed I could simply go and get help and stop worrying then this was a wake-up call. I couldn't let my guard down. Ever. I had to accept that I would always be at risk and that I shouldn't lose heart when I weakened. All I could do was keep on going and take it one day at a time.

Raining Men

As I picked my way through the VIP dining area backstage at Earl's Court on the night of the Brits 2001, I could sense I was getting a reaction. There were gasps of disbelief as I walked past the tables of the crème de la crème of the British music industry. What was going on? I know I'd been away a while but they couldn't be that surprised to see me. Perhaps they were still in shock about my performance with the inflatable legs last year. Or, maybe, Bridget Jones style, I had the back of my skirt tucked into my knickers and I was treating them to an impromptu floorshow. What was going on?

The answer turned out to be more straightforward. After almost a year away, people didn't recognise me any more because in their eyes, I had reappeared with a brand new body. Since I had started recovery and stopped bingeing I had lost weight. I knew that, but to me the changes had been gradual. To everybody else it looked like there'd been an overnight transformation. They couldn't believe that buxom Ginger and the girl making her way backstage that night were the same person. How had that happened?

My expectations for the Brits 2001 were low. I did see the event as a mini-comeback after a little while away but, as my diary entry that morning shows, I had other things on my mind.

Monday 26th February 2001

I have stopped counting days of abstinence, wonder how long its been?

Its the day of the Brits. Where was I a year ago? nervous as hell. I vomited and binged all that show. Its amazing how feelings fade tear day. Things that matter today - even if I fall down the stairs on the way to present the award - wont matter in a year, 18 months or when Im 80.

I want to make commitment of not bingeing or overeating at the Brits or all day. I am a little nervous in anticipation. It might be one big anticlimax but something usually happens, you never know.

My one and only job for the evening was presenting the Best British Male Award. All I had to do was walk down the stairs to the stage without mishap and come up with something to say once I reached the podium. It was smart thinking by the Brits panel to choose me for the job because the favourite to win Best British Male 2001 was none other than my good friend Rob and press interest in our friendship was as intense as ever. *The Daily Star* really hyped the event, claiming that 'Geri Halliwell and Robbie Williams plan to show off their love — with a passionate kiss at next week's Brit Awards'. I don't know if anyone believed that but all eyes would certainly be on us.

The first thing I had to sort out was my outfit. I had commissioned an up-and-coming young designer to make me a little beaded top for the show but he had taken forever and when it finally turned up, it wasn't worth the wait. I tried the top on the night before and it felt like a piece of cloth just hanging there, giving me no support. There was no way I was going to wear it but there was no time to get anything new. My only option was to dig through my wardrobe for something else. In the end I settled for this little gold and silver backless top, shaped like a butterfly, which I had bought in a trashy store in Miami. It wasn't exactly designer but it was better than the new one and it went with my little skirt and knee-length cream boots. It would have to do.

My next worry was what I was going to say when I got up on stage to present the award. On the morning of the ceremony, I was going through my workout with Torje trying to think up funny lines. I wanted to poke fun at the obsessive press speculation about my relationship with Rob and make people laugh. Torje made some very witty suggestions but I thought they might be a bit too risqué. Maybe I could say something that played on the title of the award itself. Surely I could get something funny out of Best British Male?

Rob had an amazing record at the Brits. He had nine already and was nominated for four more this year. When we got to our dressing rooms he was pretty relaxed and took me aside to calm my nerves. 'Geri,' he said, looking into my eyes, 'at the end of the day, it's only a TV show.' There was a really positive vibe that night and it was obvious Rob was going to win big. I was looking forward to being part of it.

As the show got under way I went for a little walkabout in the dining area where the music-industry suits and lots of the stars were tucking into their three-course meal. That was when the reaction started. I knew lots of people at the show and I can't deny it was a thrill when people came up to me saying things like 'Oh my God, you look great' and 'Wow, what a difference' but I didn't want to let the compliments go to my head. The really important thing for me was that I felt comfortable in my own skin and at ease with my body. That was something new.

I was up next, so I hurried back to my dressing room to check on my hair and make-up. I still hadn't made up my mind what I was going to say. As I waited backstage for Ant and Dec to introduce me, I decided I'd just say something nice about Rob and then play it by ear about whether to use one of Torje's naughty but funny lines. Finally Ant (or was it Dec?) built me up to the crowd and called me out on stage.

'Miss Geri Halliwell!'

As I appeared, the noise and applause was deafening. It seemed like the entire hall was going through the same reaction as the people in the VIP area.

'You look great!' said Dec (or Ant!) so I thanked him, smiled demurely and got on with reading the nominations while video clips of the different artists were shown to the audience. Then came my big moment:

'He's very male,' I started, busking it, 'he's very healthy, he's a talented artist, he's got the biggest heart and according to the press, he's giving me one, so let me return the favour by giving him one. My dearest friend Robbie Williams!'

The place went crazy as Rob got up to collect his award. Torje's joke had gone down well and there was a huge outpouring of goodwill towards Rob. I handed him the award and gave him a hug. *Daily Star* readers must have been disappointed because a snog wasn't on the agenda but it was a lovely moment and I was really happy to share it with such a great friend. Rob went on to win another two awards that evening, taking him to a record-breaking twelve Brits. I was really proud of him.

Tues 27th February 2001
Last night did the Brits. Went well. Stayed at Rob's, played cards, ate a curry and cuddled. Just lovely, it's almost funny how the press can get it so wrong. I feel blessed to have his support. Great night.

Of course the next day's papers were full of Rob's success, my body, *that* joke and more speculation about our relationship. We had both started to see the funny side of this madness but the press just wouldn't let go of the 'story'. Perhaps it is impossible for people to imagine that Rob and me could be friends, hang out together, even share a bed without there being a romantic relationship going on. The fact is that our relationship was intense and close because of all we had in common and we weren't embarrassed to cuddle or sit up all night talking. It was as close a relationship as it is possible to have, without there being a romance, so I can see why people jumped to conclusions.

I could also understand why people were so curious because I used to be the same before I was famous. I enjoyed the rumour, the speculation and the fantasy about the lives of celebrities and followed the ups and downs of Madonna's marriage to Sean Penn and the Charles and Di saga as closely as anybody. I don't blame the man and woman in the street for looking at a juicy story in the newspaper because even now, I can be tempted to do the same thing. It is more difficult to enjoy, though, when you have been on the receiving end. It makes you really aware that these are real people. I know from my own experience that when I am unfairly criticised or lied about it hurts. It's an ongoing struggle for me to ignore the comments and gossip in the newspapers and not let their words spoil my day. These days, I try to avoid the papers altogether to protect myself, rather than run the risk.

Rob loves winding the media up when he is interviewed and, in the spring of 2001, he was quoted as saying that we were friends who enjoyed 'the occasional shag'. The quote was obviously taken up by the press and blown out of all proportion. I thought it was a joke — a laddish and silly joke maybe, but just a joke. How many times has a guy said that about a girl when it's not true? I just saw it as boyish boasting but obviously it would be taken literally by the press and spread all over the newspapers. That was upsetting and I told him so.

A few days later Rob was back in the papers in a more sensible frame of mind, this time apologising. 'I must come clean,' he said. 'I have to make amends to Geri. We've never slept together. I kind of made it up as a joke. It's just me and my loose mouth.' And that's the truth. I won't defend Rob for saying something daft like that but I won't tell him off either. We've all said things we regret.

One night, not long after the Brits, I was over at Rob's house sitting on the sofa flicking between channels when I saw a ghost staring at me from the TV screen. She was wearing a white and red Adidas crop top and a red ribbon in her hair and she was looking straight at the camera with wide eyes and a smile saying, 'I wanna be a pop star.'

'Oh my God,' I called to Rob, 'you've got to come and see this.'

We sat there for the next hour watching a documentary called *Raw Spice*. It featured material shot by the Spice Girls' original management team of us rehearsing and living together in 1994. I had no idea that the programme would be on TV and felt a sort of sick excitement when I realised what we were about to see.

Without warning, I was watching myself and the other girls as we had been seven years earlier — before fame, before the split, before all of this. It was so poignant to see us struggle through our scales and fluff our lines. One scene showed me and Mel B squabbling over a harmony line that I'd messed up, another showed me desperately trying to keep up with the other girls during a dance routine. At one point I look directly at the camera and declare, 'I'm so ambitious. I wanna get my ego fed, I think. I'm quite hungry for fame.' Looking in my eyes, I could see a young girl, less than a year after losing her dad, desperate to reach her dream before time ran out.

It was so weird because the whole film was full of references to Take That and particularly to Rob.

'I can't believe it,' I said cringing, 'I never even *liked* Take That!' Rob just laughed as I sat there squirming.

Watching *Raw Spice* was an emotional experience. All of the memories came flooding back along with my feelings of love and loss for the girls. The following morning I wrote in my diary:

Wednesday 21st March 2001

Last night there was a spice girl documentary on TV. The feelings it brought up were amazing. The minga in my eyes, the pain, the sweetness of the group, the sweetness, the bittersweetness

Right now I feel quite "raw". How ironic that the name of the spice girls doc. I am going to write letters to all of the girls in gratitude. I am grateful. I feel really emotional this morning.

·

'Geri, I'm from Stoke and you're from Watford. Let's not forget that. There is *no* shame in singing 'It's Raining Men'.'

We were backstage at the Equinox Club in Leicester Square. Rob was performing a secret gig to raise money for UNICEF and we were discussing my career options. It seems ridiculous in retrospect but it took Rob's straightforward logic to convince me that my new single should be my cover version of the Weather Girls' 80s classic 'It's Raining Men'.

By January 2001 *Scream If You Wanna Go Faster* was finished and we had lined up 'Feels Like Sex' as the first single. Around this time, I got a call from a guy called Eric Fellner at Working Title who was producing the movie version of *Bridget Jones's Diary*, one of my favourite books. Eric said they were planning to use 'It's Raining Men' in the movie but wanted it to be a fresh version of the song rather than the 80s original. They knew it was very short notice, but would I consider recording it for them?

I have to admit I was flattered. The original was a camp disco classic, the movie was going to be huge and they wanted *me* to be on board. How could I refuse? Within days I found myself in the recording booth singing the words from a piece of paper. At first it was like a bad audition for *Pop Idol* — I was all over the place because I had no real idea of the words or the feel of the song but the arrangement by producer Steve Lipson really made the song work. When we played it back, we were all pretty pleased. It was great to be involved in the project and, as far as I was concerned, that was that. Until a few days later, that is, when Eric was back on the phone with a new idea. He had heard my version and he wanted it to come out as a single.

My first instinct was to say no. I thought I'd be slated if I released a cover version. What about my artistic integrity? It took Rob's more down-to-earth approach to make me realise that I was being ridiculous. Since when did I worry about whether people would think what I was doing was 'cool'? So I went to see my friends Emma Freud and Richard Curtis (who I had got to know when we were involved in Comic Relief a few years earlier and who had co-written the screenplay to *Bridget Jones*) at their home in Notting Hill to discuss the idea of the single. Emma was sitting in the bay window of her living room as I arrived and the first thing she said as I walked in was, 'Geri, if you release this record as a single it is going to be your biggest hit. It's going to be a smash.' She seemed so sure that my instinct told me to go for it.

My inspiration for the 'It's Raining Men' video came one Sunday afternoon during the regular meetings of what I call the Serenity Sunday Sisterhood. The members of the sisterhood can vary but the hardcore at that time were me and two of my close London friends, Kit and Mil. The idea was that every Sunday afternoon we would relax, order a nice take-out, watch a few silly videos and be girly. Our favourite pastime was beading — making jewellery from different coloured beads for friends — and we could just spend hours and hours doing it. I found it relaxing because I could switch off and feel normal, hanging out with my mates. This particular afternoon we decided to have an eighties musical double bill of *Fame* and *Flashdance* and as we watched the movies, I started thinking how much fun it would be to go back to the era of leg-warmers and leotards for the video.

The directors, Jake and Jim, wanted to make the video as similar in feel to the classic films that had inspired me as they possibly could. In practice that meant trying to replicate the amazing performance of Jennifer Beal from the audition scene in *Flashdance*. I had a lot of work to do — it was like a crash course in the performing arts.

The first step in the process was training. I always tended to over-exercise for a video or performance but this time I was focusing on toning my body rather than burning off fat in an uncontrolled way. In the original scene Jennifer Beal is wearing a swimsuit, but I wanted to go for a sexier look. A black bra-top and skimpy knickers was the look I was after but it meant that even more of my body would be on show. This was as revealing as it got so I worked very, very hard to get the body I wanted.

The next phase was learning the dance moves. I had always seen myself as heavy and ungraceful (whatever the truth of my size at any given point) so I felt like I had to change my whole way of working with my body. The work I did with Luca on the opening sequence was gruelling and that famous line from *Fame* kept running through my head: 'Fame costs, and right here's where you start paying ... in sweat!'

The shoot itself was the most difficult of my career by a long way. I felt like I was being stretched to my limit and, although it was very hard work, it felt great to be able to rise to the challenge. I was pulling off moves I would never have believed myself capable of. I learned to do the splits and the side-splits as well as the rock 'n' roll moves where I was being thrown in the air. I have to admit that we used a body double for the back flips but I didn't feel too bad about it because we actually had to bring in acrobats to pull that off!

The final scene takes place out in the street in the pouring rain, just like the classic *Fame* routine. It was pretty late on a freezing cold night by the time we were ready to shoot but when it started to snow we had to hold on for another two hours until it stopped. Finally, in the early hours, we turned on the rain machine and got ready to start. The fake rain was absolutely freezing but I had to forget about that and get through the routine, remember the words *and* make it look like I was having fun. Thankfully, I got it right first time and we could all go home and dry off!

All the pain felt worth it when I saw the final video. I was blown away. Somehow Jake and Jim had managed to take me right back to the 1980s and onto the set of one of my favourite TV shows. The whole project — from recording the song to making the video — had been done in an insane hurry but fantastic teamwork had allowed us to pull it off. The wonderful thing was that, within weeks it seemed, something of an eighties revival kicked in and this was perfect for it. I am very thankful for 'It's Raining Men'. I got very lucky.

If the Brits 2001 got some people talking about the way that my body had changed, then the video for 'It's Raining Men' sparked a full-blown debate. Was I anorexic? What diet was I on? Was yoga responsible? Although the initial reaction had been positive — a sort of national 'Wow!' — pretty soon the headlines changed from GERI'S TOP OF THE FIT PARADE to SHRINKING SPICE. In the end, the issue boiled down to one question: How did Geri do that?

Answering that question truthfully in the early months of 2001 was not easy because I wasn't ready to reveal that I had found help. Gradually, though, as I have made progress, I have realised how important it is to set the record straight. I have learnt that the key to sustained weight loss is realising one simple lesson and if you take one thing from reading this book, please let it be this:

DIETS DON'T WORK.

I have spent my adult life obsessing about my weight and my size. I have devoted so much energy to attempting to control the food I eat because, like most of us, I thought that eating less or cutting certain foods out of my diet was the best way to lose weight. I was wrong. It didn't matter whether I was cutting back on carbohydrates or living for days on pieces of melon, SlimFast and Müller Light — none of these diets worked for me. I don't mean that I didn't see short-term results because I did. Often, when I starved myself in the run-up to a video shoot or public appearance I would be rewarded with a skinny body, but the point is it never, ever lasted! By restricting the food that I ate to lose weight, I was just setting myself up for another full-blown binge on chocolate, cakes and biscuits. The result? I would put the weight back on and have to go back to the starvation diet all over again.

It's obvious when you think about it, but after all the bingeing I was doing in LA at the end of 2000, I really started to put on weight. Normally there were long intervals between my binges but in LA, just like in St Paul's in the autumn of 1999, my life had become one constant binge. As a result, I couldn't do my usual trick of exercising it all off the next day. My exercise regime, however gruelling, couldn't keep up with the amount I was eating and I started to gain the pounds. So I have to admit that this played its part in convincing me to take action. That may be the wrong motivation, but part of me picked up the phone and asked for help so that I could lose weight.

I was aware enough to know that I wouldn't get better if I carried on starving myself, so I tried to change my day-to-day eating habits. I came off the Dr Atkins diet and started to eat three square meals a day. It felt like a revelation to rediscover the joys of the potato! At the same time, I was exercising as hard as I ever had to prepare for the 'Raining Men' video. Pretty soon I started to see the effects — dramatic weight loss combined with a toned and muscular body. I couldn't believe it. In my eyes, I was eating more day-to-day than ever before and yet I was losing weight at the same time! Just in time for the Brits. I thought that I had finally cracked it, but as a diary entry from early February seems to hint, I was still obsessing.

> Thurs 8th february 2001.
> I am losing weight I am 6 stone 9
> (under 45 kilos) very light, but my
> anorexic head thinks 'great just a little more.
> just a little more just for the shoot.'
> my weight is freaking me out, cant believe
> Im losing it. fear of putting it back on.

By stopping my bingeing I was finally reaping the benefits of my exercise regime and the fat was falling away but 'my anorexic head' was still strong. Three meals a deal, including potatoes, is all very well but only if they are proper-sized meals. In reality it was the same old story. I still wasn't eating enough. The only difference was that this time, instead of not eating carbs or starving myself for a few days, I was eating the right foods, I just wasn't eating anything like enough of them. Looking back, it's not too difficult to understand why I succumbed to temptation when I got off the flight from Miami that time.

Breaking my abstinence was the beginning of the process of really learning my lesson. It made me realise I had to ditch the diets and eat three healthy, good-sized meals a day. Anything less and it was just a matter of time until my next binge. After years where my relationship with food was so distorted, I had to literally relearn how to eat properly. I took it each meal at a time, like little baby-steps, until I had gradually found a new regime that would allow real recovery. These days, I always have a carbohydrate, a protein and at least one vegetable on my plate and each different part of the meal is at least as big as a fist in size. I don't do diets any more — healthy eating is what keeps me slim.

I am sure many people who read the newspapers or see me on the TV assume that I am as thin as I am because I am starving myself. In reality, I am eating more food more regularly and more healthily now than I have in my entire adult life. At five foot one and a half (that half inch matters!) I am naturally a quite small person, just like my mum. The irony is that if I had just allowed my body to find its natural balance, I would have reached the comfortable weight and size I am now a long time ago.

•

As 2001 got underway I was very optimistic about the chances of another Number One single with 'It's Raining Men'. I'd made an impact at the premiere of *Bridget Jones's Diary* in early April when I gave my spare movie ticket to a kid in the crowd and invited him to be my date for the evening! Personally, though, I'd suffered a setback which had thrown my day-to-day life into chaos.

Towards the end of March, Mil, Kit and I had gone for a girly weekend to the Ritz Hotel in Paris. We had a fantastic time enjoying the luxurious setting and going shopping for clothes. We all loved the Ritz and I remember joking that I could get used to living in a hotel full time. We made the most of our time and really packed everything that we could into the weekend. We caught the Eurostar home late on the Sunday night and were all pretty tired by the time we arrived at Waterloo station. Calvin my driver was waiting to take us back to my place in Notting Hill.

He pulled up outside the entrance of the building and the three of us climbed out of the car and hurried inside, knackered and glad to be home. When I arrived at the front door of the flat, I couldn't make sense of what I saw. The door was open and there was a shoe lying abandoned in the middle of the hallway.

'That's funny,' I said, half-turning towards Kit. 'It's not like Mary not to clean up properly.'

Then I walked inside and went into the kitchen. There was some kind of purple liquid which looked like Ribena splattered all over the walls. What the hell was going on? Had the washing machine exploded and sprayed dye everywhere? Then I turned around and saw the most disgusting and vicious obscenities scrawled all over the wall and the penny dropped. Someone had broken into the flat.

I was in a daze. I couldn't really take in what had happened. I was shaken and upset but too shocked to cry or feel any fear. I wanted to know what else these people had done, so I ran upstairs to my bedroom. It was complete chaos — my clothes had been thrown all over the floor and there was purple liquid sprayed everywhere. The photograph frames on the dressing table were turned face down and one of me with Rob was missing. The violent obscenities on the wall in my room made it clear that the intruders knew perfectly well whose flat this was. Someone very angry had been in there and I knew I had to get out.

I felt as if I had been violated and my sweet little London flat didn't feel like home any more. That mattered more than the jewellery and electrical goods they had stolen. My mind raced, trying to find reasons for the attack. Why would someone want to do this to me? Was this someone with a personal grudge or just a particularly nasty burglar? A few weeks earlier, the *News of the World* had published a stupid story saying I'd chosen the flat so I could be nearer to Rob's house. I was used to this kind of nonsense but this story was more difficult to laugh off because they had printed a photograph of the street that was basically a road map to my front door. From that Sunday onward,

I had people banging on the door and abusing me over the intercom. I had tried to ignore the problem, assuming it would go away eventually, but now someone had broken in and destroyed my home. Was this the price I had to pay for fame?

I have learnt that going into denial is wrong but sometimes it can feel like the most sensible thing to do, so I decided to move out immediately and spare myself more upset. By the end of the night I had moved into the Lanesborough Hotel in the West End and I never returned. I'd lost my home and though a hotel wasn't ideal, I was grateful I could afford to get out so quickly. At least there I felt safe.

Not long after I moved into my new 'home' at the Lanesborough, Matthew Freud called with some news. I had received an intriguing offer — from the Labour Party who wanted me to star in the first Party Election Broadcast of their 2001 campaign.

For someone who could comfortably write what she knows about politics on the back of a postage stamp, I have quite a track record in British party politics! In 1996 the Spice Girls gave a tongue-in-cheek interview to the political magazine *The Spectator* in which I said Mrs Thatcher was the original Spice Girl. The fuss from the story was ridiculous and the press tried to mark me down as a true blue Tory. The truth was that politics wasn't really my thing but my dad had been a passionate Conservative and his admiration for the Iron Lady had rubbed off on me.

Like many people, I don't really have a grasp of the detail of politics and policies, so I look to the leader of a political party first and foremost. I suppose I try to get an idea of what kind of person they are and make my judgement from there. When I started to take notice of Tony Blair I must admit that I liked what I saw but it was Cherie who made an impression on me first. I met her at the launch of Breast Cancer Awareness week in September 2000. The charity launch was packed with photographers and they all wanted to get a picture of the ex-Spice Girl and Cherie. They asked us to pose on the stage together for what seemed like an eternity.

'I'm not sure how much longer I can hold this expression,' I said to Cherie, giggling through my fixed grin.

The two of us hit it off immediately. I loved her sense of humour and warmth and it was obvious to me that she has a good heart. I remember thinking how well it reflected on Tony to be married to such a fantastic woman. At the end of the event when we said goodbye, Cherie said, 'You must come to Chequers, Geri,' and promised she'd be in touch.

It wasn't until March 2001 that I had the chance to sit down and talk to the other half of the partnership. I was at the Pride of Britain Awards at the Park Lane Hilton Hotel in London when I found myself sitting next to Tony at lunch. We didn't have a very deep chat and we didn't even talk about politics. He told me about when he used to play guitar in a band. On a personal level, I really liked him. The quality I noticed when I met Tony face to face was the same thing that I had liked about him when I saw him making speeches or explaining tough decisions — he seemed to be compassionate. I don't know enough about the rights and wrongs of his policies to make a judgement but I can't think of a more important characteristic in a prime minister than compassion.

So when Matthew told me about the call from the Labour Party, I was proud to be asked but puzzled about why I had been chosen. I was willing to back Labour in the election if I was asked but I wasn't really sure that I could offer much to a Party Election Broadcast and I didn't want to get dragged into an argument about politics that I didn't really understand.

As it turned out, what they had in mind for me didn't involve complicated policy issues. Their first campaign film of the election would focus on the government's achievements in office and they just wanted me to do a little walk-on cameo. The point of my part was to illustrate the introduction of free TV licences to pensioners (which seemed like a good idea to me) and all I had to do was bring some tea in for two old ladies who were watching telly in their living room. The filming was to take place in the front room of a house in west London. The joke was supposed to be that the two women were so engrossed in watching one of my videos, they didn't even notice me when I came in with their drinks and said 'Tea's ready!'

It should have been simple. The problem was that the two women weren't actors but party supporters and they were so naturally polite that they couldn't stop themselves saying 'Ooh, thank you' whenever I arrived with their cuppas. We must have shot the scene a dozen times before they got it right and in the end it took something like two hours to get 30 seconds of film.

Once it had got out that I had taken part in the film, I was bombarded with questions by every journalist I met, trying to catch me out on my political opinions. I thought the best way of dealing with that potential banana skin was to just admit that I knew nothing about politics but thought Tony was the best man on offer for the job.

While Tony Blair had his popularity contest to win, I was busy with my own. 'It's Raining Men' was up against teen pop band S Club 7 for the Number One spot. If I made it to the top for a fourth time as a solo artist that would make it eleven Number Ones — the most ever achieved by a female singer.

Tues 1st May 2001.

10am. So today I find out my midweek, oh shit, I am quite excited and nervous. I cant wait really. I would be very surprised if its not number one. I think it deserves to be but we will see.

1.30 am So I am 10,000 ahead of Sclub7. looks like I am going to be number one! Hurrah. Phew. I don't want to miss the success this time round. I was so busy throwing up last time.

Sunday 6ᵗʰ May 2001.
feel really proud of myself, I am the most successful queen of pop.!! number ones!! and I am eating my three meals. All is well with Geraldine and Ger, Halliwell.

And by the way, a few weeks later, Tony won his race too.

If I wanted to get better, I had to look at every aspect of my life and try and understand the part it played in triggering or aggravating my eating disorder. I knew that the pressures of my job made me more vulnerable and, in the summer of 2001, I was about to go back out on the promotional circuit and expose myself to those risks all over again.

It wasn't just the pressures of photo shoots or travel that I had to worry about, I also had to recognise that my emotional wellbeing was sometimes too closely linked to the success or failure of my career. I was very excited about the release of my second album *Scream If You Wanna Go Faster* because I was so proud of it. My favourite song on the album was 'Calling', and the minute I recorded the demo of the song, I rushed over to George's house in London and played it to him. George will only offer praise if he really thinks it's deserved. He is brutally honest and it can be hard to take, but I was so confident about this song that I was willing to risk it. I stood there waiting for his verdict as the song played until, as the last noted faded, he said, 'You know what, Geri, that's very good.' From George Michael that means something. I really believed I had a winner.

In April, excited by the finished album, I wrote:

Wednesday 25th April 2001
I have such high expectations, I really want
my album to go to number one.
I want everything I do to be perfect.
I am so tired to feeling like the clumsy fuck up
especially with the Spice Girls that I want to be
great now but I need to remind myself of my rock
bottom, overeating because then I will eat properly.
I need to remind myself where the driveway
leads me to - eating out of a dustbin. The minute
I start cutting back I am on my way to a binge.

Reading those words back, it is easy to see the connection I was making between the success of my record and the need to remain abstinent. I loved the album and I wanted it to do very well, which was only natural. But what if it didn't? Would that make me the 'clumsy fuck-up' again? As the release date approached things weren't looking good — I had competition from big album-selling acts Bon Jovi and REM. In my diary I tried to prepare myself for the worst:

Tuesday 15th May 2001.
I am scared that my chart position will decide
my self esteem. maybe I'm terrified of failure
because success defines who I am.
I want it all to be perfect but maybe
the chart success that is not going to be
is something that I have to live through.

Living through it and accepting it was easier said than done. As I feared, when the album came out a week later, it only managed Number Five in the album charts. The disappointment hit me hard. I was so proud of the record that I wanted the progress I had made to be recognised. The way it was looking, though, it wasn't even going to be heard. In fact, 'It's Raining Men', a cover version I'd recorded in an afternoon, looked like being the most well-known song on it. As I toured the world promoting the album, staying 'clean' was a constant battle:

> *Wednesday 6th June 2001*
> *I was so closed to bingeing last night. I thought I was "safe in bed" but I woke up and felt so compulsive. I had this whole conversation in my head about ordering room service, junking it. ordering hot milk and apple which I was definitely eaten compulsively as I ate it down to the core.*
>
> *I am living with this compulsive monster that doesn't want to shut up. Constant nagging, whispering in my ear, like a devil "go on take some try some." It won't let up lately I wish it would. I have no control over this beast the only control I have is to make this healthy head stronger and stronger so I can have inner strength to not summit to its evil clutches.*

Just a few days later on my way home from a charity benefit in Toronto, the devil won out.

I was exhausted when I boarded the plane and during the long flight all my willpower disappeared. I ordered as much food as I could from the stewardess and pigged out. It was back to square one. I had been told that if I really wanted to get better I should avoid excessive travel, overwork, loneliness and pressure — all the things, in fact, that dominated my life through that early summer of 2001.

Did I want really want to live this way any more?

It had taken me eight years but, finally, on a warm summer's day last July, I allowed myself to grieve for my dad. I was back at the cemetery where his ashes had been scattered, for the funeral of Steve's dad, my Mum's father-in-law. Early on the morning of the service I decided to go ahead of the rest of the family to spend some time sitting and remembering Dad.

I had never been able to handle the depth of pain I felt about losing my father. Before the Spice Girls came along I was overcome by my grief but unable to express it. Afterwards I was so consumed by the group and my success that most of the time I was able to bury my pain. When I couldn't control those feelings, I used food to suppress them. Now, without my eating disorder to fall back on, the time had come to give them full reign.

I sat down on a park bench near the spot where we had scattered his ashes and let my mind fill with memories. I thought about our secret trips to the sweet shop when I was a kid and remembered trailing around car boot sales looking for bargains in the last few years of his life. I thought about the times he'd been loving and the times he'd been distant. I thought about how much had happened in the eight years since he'd gone which we had not been able to share and all the things that I could never say to him. As I sat there overlooking the gravestones and flowers, I could feel the grief and loss welling up inside me until the tears poured out, leaving me rocking back and forth on the bench absolutely howling with grief for the dad I missed so much.

I could hear his voice inside my head that morning saying, 'You've got to stop doing all your work for me, Geri. You've got to do it for yourself.' After his death I had followed my dreams of fame partly because I wanted to repay his faith in me. Now he was telling me to move on and stop living my life for his ghost. So if I wasn't chasing fame for Dad any more, then who was I chasing it for?

Was fame still what I wanted?

I had reached a turning point.

Letting go of some of the pain I felt about losing my dad made me realise that I could stop running if I wanted to. For the first time I could really question the addiction to fame and celebrity that had driven me for so long.

Saturday 1st September 2007

I need to emotionally let go of fame celebrity
It needs to have even less power over me
Although it has less than it ever did
I need to work on this so I am not a slave to it.
Nothing last forever. I think I am not that bad
on it anymore, but one never knows.

I never want to appear ungrateful for fame and celebrity and all that it has given me but I have learned that I can't let that desire run my life. A month after I told my diary that I didn't want to be a slave to fame any more, I got a glimpse of how it would feel to be its master.

For me, performing live has always been the most nerve-wracking but most exhilarating part of what I do. Although I had plenty of experience in front of big audiences, after the Spice Girls I'd only ever appeared as part of a big show with lots of other acts. I didn't know if I could carry a show by myself but I wanted to find out by playing somewhere low-key and out of the way where I wouldn't attract too much attention. So early last summer I called Andy to see if he had any ideas. It didn't take him long to call back with a solution.

'Geri,' he said, 'I've found the perfect thing. The Ministry of Defence want you to play to the troops in Oman in the Gulf. They are doing exercises out there and they could do with some entertainment and are planning a concert at the end of October.' It was a long way to go and hardly the typical gig but that was why it was so perfect. No one would bother me and very few people would be watching. I agreed and half forgot about it — back in June, October seemed a long way off.

On the afternoon of September 11th I was working in a TV studio in London on my yoga video. The paparazzi photos that had appeared of me practising my yoga moves on holiday with Rob and later on a trip to Italy in 2001 had created a lot of interest in the subject and I'd been invited to make a video with my new teacher Katy. We abandoned filming that afternoon as the pictures started to come through on the TV news. Like everybody else I was completely shocked by the horrific images of the World Trade Center.

When the world changed that afternoon, my quiet low-key concert for the soldiers in Oman changed too. We were now on the brink of war and these troops, in the heart of the troubled region, could be called upon at any moment. They were also prime targets. Soon after the attacks Mum phoned begging me to cancel the concert and even Andy was nervous about the trip. I listened to what they said about the uncertainty of the situation and the risks of going to such a volatile region but right from the beginning I believed it would be wrong to change my plans.

The army had organised the concert to raise the morale of the troops. Surely that was even more important now? Backing out would be cowardly and anyway, this was my chance to do my bit and I was proud to do the patriotic thing. As the concert approached at the beginning of October, the world was still waiting for the military response from Britain and America. I have to admit that as I boarded the flight I did feel nervous, although whether they were nerves about the political situation or the prospect of my first full-length concert was hard to tell.

The flight was long and tiring so it was a relief when we arrived in Oman. The Wing Commander assigned to look after me for the trip met us at the airport and we were driven to a hotel in the capital, Muscat, where I was staying. Fame has taken me to the most fabulous hotels in the world in the last five years but I can honestly say that the Crown Suite at the Grand Hyatt in Muscat was the grandest, most over-the-top and indulgent of them all.

I won't deny that I enjoy a bit of luxury but the suite I was taken to in Muscat was beyond ridiculous. As I walked in the door I could hardly believe what I saw. The living room was like a Sultan's palace.

Chandeliers hung from a ceiling that was panelled in something that looked very much like gold! An enormous picture window opened onto a huge balcony overlooking the Gulf of Oman and in the corner there was a full-size, jet-black grand piano. Next, the hotel manager showed me round the master bedroom (there were three bedrooms in all) with its grand four-poster bed, leopard-skin chaise-longue, bathroom, Jacuzzi *and* sauna en-suite. I felt honoured but a little overwhelmed too. I couldn't believe all this splendour was for me. As it turns out, the luxury was not to last too long. The next morning things got a lot more military.

The plan was for the whole group — me and my team, the support act Steps and the compere Bobby Davro — to fly to the Salahah beach resort which was closer to the concert venue at a place called Camp South. The heat was already intense as we arrived at the airbase that morning. I didn't know anything about army transport, so I hadn't really thought about how we'd be getting from A to B. I got a bit of a shock when I realised we would be flying in an enormous Hercules troop carrier.

As we settled into the makeshift seats at the side of the aircraft, the engines started to rumble into life and the whole plane shook as it set off down the runway. Take-offs are always a scary experience but this was the noisiest and most frightening I'd ever been through and it didn't get much better once we were airborne — it was a very bumpy ride. My hotel suite might have been luxurious but this was as rough and ready as it got. I was in the army now and I had better get used to it!

Halfway through the flight, the Wing Commander leant over and asked me if I wanted to have a look in the cockpit. I jumped at the chance to check out the view and say hello to the pilots.

After I'd been there for a couple of minutes the Captain turned to me and said, 'Well, Geri, how would you like a go at flying this thing?'

'Are you serious?' I said.

'Absolutely,' he replied, moving from his seat to let me in. 'Sit down.'

I thought it was all a big joke as I sat there being given a five-minute lesson on how to pilot a military aircraft. It was nice of them to indulge me but I was pretty certain the co-pilot was doing the driving. But then, as I held onto the controls, my back tensed and I realised that the weight of the engine was in my hands. I still couldn't believe that they'd really let me fly the plane, so I eased the control to the left and, as I did, the whole plane veered with me. This was no joke — I was in control of the plane and for a quarter of an hour they let me stay there. It was one of the most terrifying and exciting experiences of my life. I'm not sure Steps and Bobby Davro were so happy, though, because I wasn't the steadiest pilot in the world. I don't know if they all managed to hold onto their breakfast!

We arrived at the beach resort in sweltering 90 degree heat. The beach was one of the most beautiful I have ever seen but the resort was absolutely swarming with paparazzi. The heat was so oppressive that I couldn't allow myself to worry about the possible pictures so I went down to the beach to sunbathe and have a swim before returning to the hotel. As usual, I had left my rehearsing to the last minute and we had work to do. Tomorrow was the show and we had a whole set to perfect.

I spent Saturday working on my routines with Luca and my team of dancers at the hotel in Salahah. I wanted to rehearse until the very last minute to make sure everything was right but, eventually, the knock came from the Wing Commander to tell us it was time to go. If flying the Hercules was one of the most extraordinary experiences of my life, sitting up on the flight deck on the Chinook military helicopter that flew us to the venue comes a close second. The sun was setting as we took off and the orange light and growing darkness made the journey through the mountains and desert extraordinarily dramatic. It felt unreal, like some kind of computer game, as the aircraft swooped down over the sand towards the site. In the distance, I could see an enormous hill with a floodlit stage at its summit. This was 'Halliwell Hill', constructed for the night by the Royal Engineers. As we approached I looked out of the side window and saw men in their desert khaki approaching from every direction. Six thousand soldiers on their way to Halliwell Hill.

In fact, the music was not the only entertainment that night. First of all there was the small matter of England's crucial World Cup qualifier against Greece which was being shown on an enormous screen in front of the stage. While the boys were watching the game, I waited in the makeshift tent that served as backstage to prepare myself for the performance. My usual nerves had started to kick in but they were about to get worse. On the other side of the tent, 6,000 troops were more than a little drunk and growing very tense — England were losing.

And then David Beckham came to the rescue.

There were just seconds to go and the mood was ugly in the crowd. England were about to crash out of World Cup qualification and I was going to have to play to a group of very pissed off — and very pissed — soldiers. Then, like a miracle, there was the most enormous cheer from the crowd behind me. Beckham had saved England and rescued the party with a wonder goal! Thanks, David!

Now, though, there was a new problem. I'm not sure which is worse, a crowd turning ugly or a completely overexcited one. I could hear Bobby Davro up on stage calling for order: 'PLEASE STOP PUSHING!' he was shouting. 'MOVE BACK! SOMEONE'S GOING TO GET HURT.' I was starting to get worried that the whole thing was getting out of hand. After all, these guys had been stuck in the middle of nowhere for weeks and were facing an uncertain future. No wonder they were letting off steam.

Finally the time came for me to get out there and perform. Up to this point I hadn't actually seen the crowd but, from the side of the stage, wearing a black leather coat and a tiny pair of knickers, I peeked out and saw this vast, swaying mass of testosterone roaring in anticipation of the show. Luca was beside me, sensing my nerves. 'Geri,' he said, 'you're going to have to go out there now, but when you do make sure you get them on your side. Don't tell them off and you'll be alright.' Then, with only moments before I had to go on, I got down on my knees and prayed.

Please God, help me get through this.

I went on stage with my team of girl dancers to 'Scream If You Wanna Go Faster' and although I could tell the crowd were going crazy I wasn't sure what sort of crazy it was. Normally we would go straight into the next song but I thought it would be best to talk to the crowd first and make sure I had them with me. As the song finished the noise was incredible.

'Hi guys,' I started. 'I just want to let you know that this is my first time doing a whole show on my own. I know you guys are gentlemen, so please be gentle with me, because you know what they say — a girl never forgets her first time.'

After that, I never looked back. I ran through my solo hits and threw in a few cover versions too. I even did a slowed down version of 'Wannabe'. And as I sang that night I could feel something happening inside. I had experienced the buzz of live performance before but this was something else. For the first time the dance steps came to me easily and I began to enjoy the routines rather than simply forcing my way through them. Once the set was in full swing, I couldn't stop smiling. I felt at ease on the stage and found myself wrapping this rowdy crowd around my little finger. As one song ended and I soaked up the applause I looked out into the audience and something dawned on me. I wasn't clumsy Geri any more.

I was good at this.

It was all a complete revelation for me. My doubts about fame and uncertainty about where my life should go next were balanced by a real sense of gratitude for the pleasure I could give and receive through what I do. I felt this even more powerfully the following day when I spent seven hours in a helicopter flying from base to base to meet the troops who couldn't get to the concert. There was no doubt that seeing a famous face lifted their spirits. They were miles from home and quite possibly in danger, so the least I could do was to try to take their minds off it all for a while. When I got home that night, the news broke that air-strikes against Afghanistan had begun.

Monday 8th October 2001

The soldiers I have met touched my life forever
when I watched CNN they weren't just little action
heroes anymore. These are real human beings
that might die, full of fear, needing love
and I felt that need yesterday.
Some of them were so young - only boys really
I was scared shitless and God knows how they
are dealing with it. Being in Oman makes it
all so real, this "war on terrorism"
I used to watch the news feeling disconnected
now it feels real.

Oman had been an unexpected gift. I felt like I had finally come into my own as a performer out there and I knew that the buzz I had felt was one addiction I never could give up. I also realised that fame is full of contradictions. For every scrape with a pushy paparazzi or nasty story in the newspapers there is something positive that makes it all worthwhile, whether it's the smile on the face of a teenage soldier or riding over the desert in a helicopter at dusk.

I had a lot to be grateful for.

Fame

The sun's dipping down below the palm trees by the pool and it's almost time to go inside. I have a support group meeting to get to down in Santa Monica and the traffic out of West Hollywood will be bumper to bumper soon. I need to make sure I attend as often as I can because, almost eighteen months after I first asked for help, it is still a day-to-day struggle for me to resist temptation.

The time I have had here in LA has given me the space I needed to understand what has happened to me since I left the Spice Girls. Four years on I am standing at a crossroads in every area of my life — my home, my relationships, my career, my fame. After Oman it took me a while to find the chance to stop and really take stock. The trip to the Gulf had reminded me of the positive side of celebrity but in the months that followed I still felt as if I was struggling with my schizophrenic relationship with fame. Part of me remained addicted to the thrill of it all but part of me wanted to escape. The moments that stand out in the months between my trip to Oman and my arrival here reflect those contradictions vividly.

Cherie Blair was true to her word. Last autumn, a year after we had met at the launch of Breast Cancer Awareness Week, an envelope marked 10, Downing Street arrived at my latest temporary home, a flat on the Chelsea embankment in London, owned by my friend Kit's mum Nina. Inside was an invitation requesting the pleasure of my company for dinner at Chequers, the Prime Minister's country residence in Buckinghamshire, on Saturday 1st December. Just as she had promised, Cherie had invited me for a meal with her and Tony. I was thrilled to have been asked and couldn't wait to get on the phone to tell my mum.

'That's wonderful, Geri,' she said. 'Now you just make sure you don't disgrace yourself.'

'Of course I won't,' I told her. 'What could go wrong?'

By the time the day arrived I was very excited but pretty relaxed. After all, Tony and Cherie had always been so nice and normal whenever I'd met them so I was just looking forward to seeing them. In fact I was so chilled out about the occasion that when I saw Harry looking up at me with his big can-I-come-too? eyes, my heart melted and I picked him up and took him with me. I didn't think Tony and Cherie would mind. It was a freezing night and after the 40 mile drive from London I was pretty anxious to get inside the warmth of the grand old country house . I can't have been as cold as Harry though because as soon as the butler opened the door he bolted out of my arms and inside. I think Tony and Cherie probably saw him before they saw me!

I was one of fifteen or so dinner guests that night including my friend Des O'Connor, the Blairs' very sweet daughter Katherine, the Olympic rower Steve Redgrave, some Lord I'd never heard of and an old rocker from the sixties whose name I could never remember (I think he was one of Tony's teenage favourites). Dinner was very nice but I didn't say a lot. In that sort of company it seemed wise to sit and listen and not try to talk.

After dinner I was determined to grab Tony. I wanted to ask him a question, so when Cherie offered to give the guests a guided tour of the house, I followed Tony into his study and plucked up the courage to ask: 'I apologise for picking your brains, but I'm probably like most of the country — I've got absolutely no idea about the Euro. Can you explain it to me?'

I felt a bit bad — this was Tony's night off after all — but he got quite into the subject. I didn't follow all the arguments but he was starting to convince me that the Euro would help Britain's trade when I suddenly smelt something. The look on Tony's face told me he did too. Then, at exactly the same moment, the pair of us looked down at the floor to see Harry staring up at us next to a fresh puddle of pee.

'I am *so* sorry,' I said, mortified at the shame of it. 'I can't believe he's done that in *here*! In your study where you do all your thinking!'

By now Tony was laughing. 'It doesn't matter,' he said. 'Don't worry about it. We'll get it cleaned up. As I was saying . . .' And then he finished telling me all about the benefits of the Euro.

When I got home that night I wrote about the evening in my diary:

Saturday 12th December 2001

Just got back from chequers. Harry did
a wee in Tonys study but he was so
nice about it. Had a lovely chat with him
about the Euro. I actually really like
him something gentle and kind in his eyes.
felt great and privileged to be in such company
with the Prime Minister and Cherie.

On nights like that, my fame seemed to be a key that opened every door. I could talk to the most powerful man in the country and quiz him on any issue I desired. This wasn't about the glamour and glitz of the red carpet, or the paparazzi, this was about the privileged access that fame alone can buy.

The problem was, as ever, that it couldn't last. My third single from *Scream* didn't do much better than my second. 'Calling' was my favourite song on the record and I hoped against hope that it would make an impact but it just seemed to fall away, only managing Number Seven in the charts. There was no escaping the fact that my recent chart performances had been disappointing but I didn't want to let it destroy me. I was trying to feel proud of my work and not worry what others thought. By not reading the newspapers I hoped to protect myself, but when you are famous it's not as easy as that.

Early one morning at the end of December, I was checking in at Heathrow for a flight to Berlin when I saw some familiar faces. Gemma and Malcolm are two of my most devoted fans. They are always waiting for me at airports and outside TV studios and they are very sweet and supportive.

'Hi,' I said, feeling exhausted but wanting to be friendly.

'Hi, Geri,' said Gemma. 'Don't believe what they are saying in the papers.'

'Yeah,' added Malcolm. 'Take no notice. We don't think you're washed up.'

I knew they meant well but their words pushed me over the edge. Washed up? Is that what they were saying? Is that what everyone actually thought about me? All my pent-up frustration and fear inside about the way *Scream* and 'Calling' had performed rose up inside. As I sat on the plane waiting for take off, I poured my heart out in my diary:

Wednesday 19th December 2007

I've just been blubbing in the toilets at the airport completely crying my eyes out. Am I really washed up? Am I over? I haven't picked up a newspaper in six months. Is everyone pretending it's all ok?

Sometimes I feel like turning away from life. Goodness knows I am so fucking minded. Can't handle pressure or the perfechanism that I force on myself until I learn to undo that ill guess ill never be happy.

However much I told myself about the dangers and the downside of fame, it was terrifying to face up to the prospect that it might one day disappear. That afternoon in my Berlin hotel room was a struggle. In my diary I wrote about the 'snack debate' that raged in my head. A year before I would have buckled under the pressure and binged, but that afternoon I managed to hold on. It made me wonder why, if this is what fame does to me, I was so scared of losing it.

·

For three weeks over Christmas and New Year I was able to escape but I had to travel 6,000 miles to Cape Town and then Zimbabwe to do it. This was my first holiday in five years without paparazzi. Hiding in trees or skulking in the bushes is a dangerous business in Cape Town. The crime problems they have there mean that people tend to shoot first and ask questions later! So I had found a place where I could give the paps the slip at last. It was an idyllic time and an opportunity to reflect.

Wednesday 2nd Jan 2002 Cape Point South Africa

I am at the point where the Indian Oceans meets the Atlantic at the lip of Africa. I am at the edge of the world pretty free. I really think its time to make some big changes in my life. I have been on this planet almost 30 years. Maybe I should do one more album and then quit or maybe I should pack up and become a pirate and live by the sea! I wonder what my future is?

I'm still wondering about that future this evening, stuck in traffic in LA on the way to my group therapy meeting. I hope I'm going to make it on time.

I wish I could say I've found all the answers but the truth is I haven't yet. I used to spend my life dreaming about the future, promising myself that I'd be happy if I got to Number One or lost another few pounds. I try not to do that any more. Maybe the most important lesson I've learned in the last year or so is that you have to live for today because tomorrow never comes.

I have made one decision already. My 'dream house' St Paul's is on the market. I had some good times there, especially when Rob, Jonny and the gang were hanging out but I can see now that it was the kind of place I thought I should live in rather than the home I needed. At the end of last year I went over to the house to pack up a few things and say my goodbyes. The dining room I'd had done out in red with an enormous table and seats for eighteen looked a bit forlorn. No wonder really — I'd only ever used it twice. I wanted to remember the good times but I left that day feeling sad. It was time to move on.

Things are less clear when it comes to my career. In a way, the 'failure' of my last single has been strangely liberating. Always wanting to be the best has been a mixed blessing for me. That drive to make it to the top has served me well (it might explain those eleven Number One records!) but it has its downside. All too often, I have linked my professional success with my self-esteem. I literally believed I was only as good as my next record.

So what happens when that record doesn't do so well? Was I going to curl up and die? Well, it hasn't killed me and it turned out I was stronger than I realised.

I am very proud of what I have achieved in my solo career. In the UK I have had four solo Number One singles and three more in the Top Ten, as well as two Top Ten albums. I have also had lots and lots of hits all over the world since I went out on my own and all those countries count too! At the beginning of the year I won the award for Best Single with 'It's Raining Men' at the French equivalent of the Brits, the NRJ Awards in Cannes. Whatever people pretend about awards, I can tell you it's a thrill when they open that envelope and announce your name. I don't want to get carried away by the glitz any more because I know it's not real and it never lasts, but that night I managed to simply enjoy myself. It was fun to dress in a nice frock and walk up the red carpet and it was lovely to be appreciated.

But in the end, I know I can't allow my self-esteem to depend on winning awards. No matter how successful you are it can't last for ever. The most important thing for me is that I love a record and am proud of it. That's still how I feel about *Scream If You Wanna Go Faster*. I think it's a better album than my first one and I want that to be my motivation in the future. Looking back at the difference between the girl that left the Spice Girls and the person I am today, I take real pride in the creative work I have done and the performer I've become. I used to be the clumsy one, hiding at the back, but over the years that has changed. Whatever I do next it will be as a performer because that's what I am and I think I'm a pretty good one too.

My ambition to try my hand at a movie role is still strong and while I've been here in Hollywood I've spoken to a few people about projects that might suit me. But I'm not rushing into anything just yet. The newspapers are still making up stories about me and the movies, just like they did back in 1998. I can honestly say that I'm not the desperate little girl rushing off to Tinseltown trying to land myself a big break in the movies that the press say I am. Hollywood is the stuff that dreams are made of and it would be great if the right thing came along for me, but if it doesn't that's OK. I am not a wannabe any more.

One thing I do want for my future is a family. As I get older the urge to have a child one day becomes stronger. I have come to realise how important it is to live life for other people as well as yourself. That's why I've taken such satisfaction from working for the UN and going out and entertaining the troops. It seems to me that the purest expression of that is the love a mother feels for her child — a love for another that is stronger than the love you feel for yourself. I am sure that I want to experience that. First of all, though, I have to find a man.

I think I'm like most women when it comes to looking for Mr Right. I have to admit that I've been pretty unsuccessful when it comes to relationships. I've been out with some interesting, stimulating and attractive guys but none of them has really been husband material. I think I have to learn to relax a little more about that too. Maybe if I stop looking for Mr Right he might walk in the door.

And if he doesn't? The other day I picked up a card for a sperm bank I'd heard about here in LA called Cyrobank.com. I haven't got to the stage where I'm ready to go and make a withdrawal just yet but I am glad to know where to go if I need to! It's always good to have a fall-back position!

And what about my future when it comes to fame itself? I suppose I want the impossible — I want to be able to pick and choose the parts I want and escape the things that drive me crazy and make me vulnerable. It doesn't work like that, though. Sometimes I can laugh about the nonsense I hear and read that other people probably think is the truth about my life. At other times it's more difficult. When it comes to fame, do I have to take the whole package or nothing at all?

Four years ago, the most important thing in my life was making it on my own. I was still chasing the sparkle of fame and dreaming of a glamorous future. Things have changed since then and now the most important thing is making sure I am healthy. Some people think getting help for an addiction is the end of the story but it's only the first step along the way. I am not pretending for a moment that recovery is an easy process but I have learned to take one day at a time. I will always have this illness and I will always have to fight it. The moment I let my guard down or feel too much stress or pressure, I know another binge could be round the corner. I still binge sometimes. I have done it here in LA. The good news is that it happens less often now, and when it does happen, it is easier to regain control and stop.

I'm almost at the meeting now. It's just a few blocks along on the left. This is getting to be a familiar drive — I came here yesterday and the day before that and I'll be back again tomorrow — and every day, slowly, I am getting stronger.

Spring 2002

what an amazing few weeks
Performed in Hollywood for George Lucas
and Steven Spielberg! Then went to

Russia for a two day trip. 'Calling'
is number one! The fans were
throwing themselves at the car.
Pretty wild. Apparently Russians
identify with the song.

Then got back to L.A. learnt that its
when you stop looking you might
just find what you want.
have just met a really nice guy!
one day at a time

love Geri xxx

Calling Barcelona September 2001

Hen Hmens changed a lot girls
Lily Lndn 2001

Kelly the big dark knight protector

Los Angeles 2002.

The only thing I regret is not trying.
Be bold be brilliant be beautiful.

what I eat? average day

morning Bowl of porridge with fruit
                    coffee e milk

lunch   Couscous, salmon or some sort
        of fish + salad (Caesar my favourite)

afternoon snack   apple + milk or carrots.

        Dinner   salad to start

chicken, mash potatos, loads of veg.
/ baked

warrior

shoulder stand

triangle

Will this salad
make me fat ??
Duh?

Sometimes I feel like mickey just a cartoon character

This book is dedicated to the walking wounded.
I hope you find peace, love and adventure.

Geri
x

I would like to thank all the special people in my life for their love, support and encouragement — Kit, Pandora, Sabrina, Anna Kate, Mil, Craig, Charlie, Pippa and Nicky, Rob Burley, Rob W, Robbie H, Janine, Kenny, George, Luca, Kim, Molly and William, Emma and Richard, Linda, Matthew, Rebecca at EMI, all the big cheeses at EMI, Briggs, Katy, Simon, Sally, Barbara, Nina, Charles, Julian, Andy, Michelle, Andy and Paul, Rick Nowels, Peter Vettese, Steve Lipson and Hef, Baggy, Dicka, Lisa, Jason and Daz, Baz and Marg, Janine, Jake Lingwood and everyone at Ebury, Michael and Grainne, friends of Bill and of course Deanie — it's all because of you!! Thanks.

Love to my gorgeous family. Mum, I love you.

EXTRA SPECIAL THANKS TO ALL MY FANS.

Geri and Dean would also like to thank all involved in the creation of the photography — in particular Andy Stephens, Michelle McGarry, John Leahy, Trudy Bellinger, Cathy Cremer, Helen Mitchem, Kim Bowen, David Thomas, Kenny Ho, Claire Frith, Mauricio Lemus, Liam Dunn, Carol Hart, Richard Bastick, Richard Brown, Toby Dodson, Toby Newman, Glen Burrows, Joe Tanis and Brad Nelson. Also thanks to Rob O'Connor (Stylorouge), Greg Jakobek-Warsaw, Ken Watts, Lisa Anderson, Nancy Phillips, Victoria Williamson, Jonathan Hackford, Luca Tomassini, Hamilton, Melanie (yoga), Gaby at Select, Terri Manduca, Mark Cumming, Catherine Lutman, Jean-Michel Dentand, Richard Poulton, Adam and Luke at Attitude and Trashy.com. Special thanks to Michael Mack and Grainne Perkins at Grace.

Dean would like to thank Helen, Becca and Alicia and Michael Anderson for all their support and dedicates his work on this project to his mother Sonny.

Dean Freeman conceived the original concept for this book in February 1999. Dean shoots for Marie Claire, Sunday Times, Glamour, Instyle and numerous celebrity and advertising clients worldwide. His work is a part of the permanent collection of the National Portrait Gallery, London. Dean originated the concept and shot all the images for the award winning number one bestseller David Beckham My World.